FERRARI
GTO
THE CLASSIC EXPERIENCE

ACKNOWLEDGEMENTS

RICHARD BIRKS
GIANNI BULGARI
ING. CARLO CHITI
ING. MAURO FORGHIERI
OLIVER GENDEBIEN
FRANCO GOZZI
BOB GROSSMAN
JEAN GUICHET
CHARLIE HAYES
HOWARD HAIGHT
PHIL HILL
INNES IRELAND
CHRISTOPHER KERRISON
MARK KONIG
FRANCO LINI
DONALD McLEOD
JOHN MECOM
JOHN MINNEY
EDWIN NILES
ROGER PENSKE
DAVID PIPER
M. ROMAN
MICHAEL SALMON
ROY SALVADORI
JACK SEARS
JOHN SURTEES
PETER SUTCLIFFE
JACQUES SWATERS
PROF. NINO VACCARELLA
COMTE. GIOVANI VOLPI DI MISURATA

PAT BENZ - Ferrari Owners Club of America
KEN BRADSHAW - Ferrari Owners Club GB.
DIDIER GRIFFE - Club Ferrari, France
ADRIENNE WATSON - British Racing
    Drivers Club

ANNICE COLLETT & LYNDA SPRINGATE
    National Motor Museum

NEIL EASON - GIBSON - R.A.C. Motor
    Sports Association

BOB McCAFFREY - L.A.T.

AUTOSPORT and MOTOR SPORT magazines
THE FERRARI 250GT COMPETITION
    CARS by Jess G. Pourret

TONY RAWLINGS

7

*"It was the most beautifully
balanced GT car - literally
a ballet dancer on four wheels"*
MICHAEL SALMON

FERRARI
GTO
THE CLASSIC EXPERIENCE

ALAN LIS

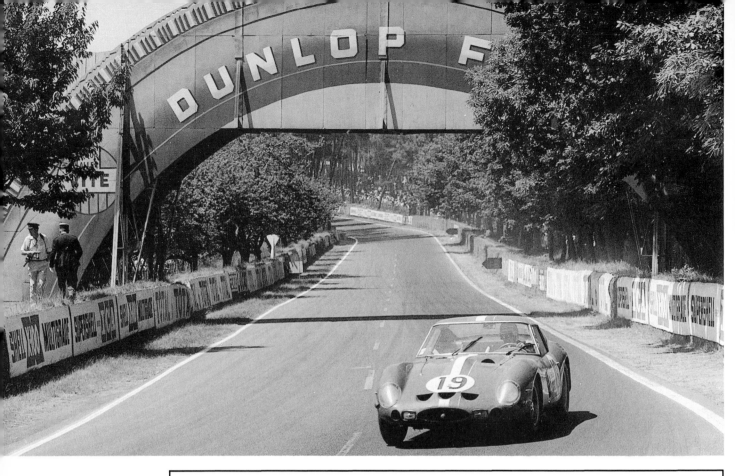

A FOULIS MOTORING BOOK

First published 1991

© RACECAR GRAPHIC 1990

Published by:
Haynes Publishing Group
Sparkford, Near Yeovil, Somerset BA22 7JJ
England

Haynes Publications Inc.
861 Lawrence Drive, Newbury Park,
California, 91320, USA

Produced for GT Foulis & Co. by
RACECAR GRAPHIC
Telephone or Fax (0935) 31295
Editorial Director: Ian Bamsey
European Editor: Alan Lis

British Library Cataloguing in Publication Data
Alan Lis

Ferrari GTO - The Classic Experience
1. Racing cars, history
I. Title
629.22809

ISBN 0-5429-839-8
Library of Congress Catalog
Card number 90-84492

Printed in England by:
J.H.Haynes & Co. Ltd.
Typesetting & Artwork by:
Photosetting, Yeovil, Somerset

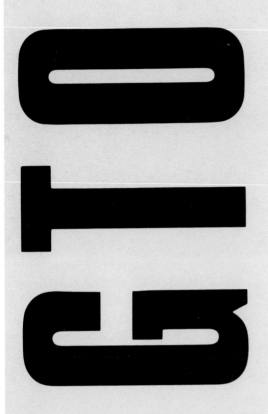

GENESIS

1962

1963

1964

POST '64

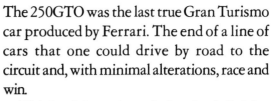

The 250GTO was the last true Gran Turismo car produced by Ferrari. The end of a line of cars that one could drive by road to the circuit and, with minimal alterations, race and win.

This book is not intended as the definitive race record of the 250GTO, nor the definitive technical analysis, both subjects that have been covered elsewhere. Rather the foundation of this book is an exclusive collection of interviews with people involved in the design, development and racing of one of the classic cars of all time.

Within these pages you will find the people who were there at the time giving their account of the GTO's merits and foibles, its victories and disasters. Some put the record straight on events erroneously recorded elsewhere while others reveal for the first time the fascinating and sometimes controversial truth behind the legend.

Given that these events happened almost thirty years ago the ability of those interviewed to recall incidents with such a wealth of detail and accuracy is remarkable.

This then is the true story of the Ferrari 250GTO as a human adventure.

The Parkes/Mairesse factory 4.0 litre GTO at the 1962 'Ring 1000Kms. Though the two regular GTOs in the race failed to finish, this car came home second overall.

The Ferraro/Scarlatti GTO on the 1962 Targa Florio. Owned by Ferraro, the car came home fourth overall and GT class winner, sporting body damage by the finish.

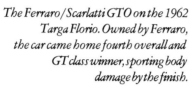

The GTO excelled at Le Mans in '62. This is the Elde/Beurlys example which finished third overall, second in class (to another GTO) at the start of the memorable race.

The Lightweight E Type was the greatest threat to the GTO in '63. Here Salvadoris Jaguar passes as Parkes refuels the Coombs GTO during the Tourist Trophy at Goodwood.

Graham Hill lifts a front wheel en route to victory in the 1963 Tourist Trophy. The car is Maranello's famous 4399 which was one of the most successful GTOs.

GENESIS

THE COLOMBO V12 ENGINE

The very first Ferrari engine was a V12 designed by Giaocchino Colombo. The ex-Alfa Romeo man began drawing in August 1945 and by the end of 1946 three of the Tipo 125 60 degree units were complete.

The 1500cc. Tipo 125 engine, so named because the capacity of each cylinder was 125cc., had a bore and stroke of 55mm. x 52.5mm. giving it, for the time, a uniquely oversquare configuration. The major castings were in a copper and aluminium alloy called Silumin with cast iron cylinder liners. A steel crankshaft machined from a solid billet was nitrided and ran in seven Vandervell thinwall main bearings each supported by a duraluminium cap, bar that which formed the lower half of the flywheel housing, which was of Silumin.

Alloy pistons with pairs of oil control and compression rings drove forged connecting rods attached by free floating gudgeon pins. The big end cap bolts - one either side of each crankshaft pin - were at a 40 degree angle to the centreline of the con rod. On each cylinder bank, in a separate head casting, was a single overhead camshaft driven by a triple row chain. The camshaft operated single exhaust and inlet valves for each cylinder, these set at an included angle of 60 degrees in a hemispherical combustion chamber. Twin hairpin springs closed each valve. A single spark plug per cylinder was located inside the vee fired by twin Marelli magnetos.

The fuel pump was driven off the nose of the camshaft on the left side while a high pressure oil pump gear driven off the camshaft circulated oil through the system via a heavily ribbed sump. The water cooling system was operated by a centrifugal pump which fed into the left cylinder bank.

Six exhaust ports exited on the outside of each head casting, while paired intake ports were fitted since the engine was intended to be supercharged for Grand Prix use. Intake pressure had been calcu-

lated to be easier to maintain with twinning. Power was quoted at 72b.h.p. at 5400r.p.m. for the GT version of the engine, while the 125 Sport motor was rated 118b.h.p. at 7000r.p.m.

Fuel supply was by three four choke Weber 30 DCF carburettors, although both three and six twin choke set-ups were also used. Under two-stage supercharged boost of 2.4 bar, the Formula One version of the engine eventually produced 315b.h.p. at 7800r.p.m.

By the end of 1950 Ferrari had come to the realisation that supercharged cars, with their high fuel consumption and the time-consuming pit stops necessitated by their thirst, could be beaten by a large capacity V12. Superior fuel efficiency allowing a car powered thus to complete a Grand Prix without refuelling while the permitted three times displacement provided plenty of power potential.

With Colombo having returned to Alfa Romeo, a 4.5 litre V12 was designed by Aurelio Lampredi. The Colombo unit was relegated to use as a sports car engine. Development nevertheless continued and over subsequent seasons of racing, larger capacity versions of the engine were built to run without supercharge. As early as 1948 a 2.0 litre type 166 version had appeared with a 60mm. bore and 58.8mm. stroke. Further increases in capacity occurred by widening the bore, while the 58.8mm. stroke remained constant. Subsequent models included a 2.3 litre Tipo 195 (65mm. bore), a 2.6 litre Tipo 212 (68mm. bore) and a 2.7 litre Tipo 225 (70mm. bore).

In 1952 the first 3.0 litre version of the engine appeared, the 250 Mille Miglia (73mm. bore). Later manifestations of this and the 166MM competition engines were equipped with individual intake porting but the paired induction tracts remained on the road-going cars. There was, however, still no sign of the twin cam heads used on the supercharged engine in 1950.

By 1956 the engine was solely in use in GT cars producing a potent 240b.h.p. at 7000r.p.m. for 3.0 litres unblown: 80b.h.p. per litre. In 1957, having ceased development of the line of Lampredi-inspired engines, a decision was taken by Ferrari to return the Colombo V12 to the battlefront of competition. In doing so a legend was born.

Ferrari's Testa Rossa version of the Colombo V12 is rightly regarded as one of the most famous and revered engines in motor sporting history. The name 'Testa Rossa' was first used in 1955 when Lampredi built a two litre four cylinder engine. To differentiate between racing examples and units for the road, cam covers were painted red. This concept soon became standard practice within the Ferrari engine range and the late Fifties V12 sports racer was known as the Red Head, or Testa Rossa.

During 1957 engineers Chiti, Rocchi and Salvarani were engaged in an intensive development programme aimed at giving the Colombo V12 a new lease of life. The bore and stroke went unchanged, as did the single camshafts. Major changes occurred elsewhere. The original angled-bolt forged con rods were replaced with more conventional rods machined from a billet of steel. The head castings were modified to provide one intake port per cylinder rather than the siamesed induction arrangement of the original.

Relocation of the spark plugs outside the vee, not only simplified plug changes but more importantly allowed the use of larger valves, allied to stronger valve springs. With suitable camshaft timing, the breathing of the engine was greatly improved.

The compression ratio was raised from 9.0:1 to 9.8:1 and running with six Weber 40 DCN twin choke carburettors the factory quoted power output was 300b.h.p. at 7,200r.p.m. The first example had wet sump lubrication but the sports racers were subsequently equipped with dry sump units sporting red cam covers...

Following a triumphant 1958 season for the Testa Rossa sports-racer, further engine changes were made. In particular, alterations to the locating stud pattern and the liners permitted the introduction of twin helical valve springs to replace the original hairpin type. Essentially the Testa Rossa V12 specification was now set for the remained of the engine's life,

though there would be detail changes such as an increase in sump capacity and relocation of ancillaries.

The Testa Rossa V12 remained a sports-racing unit until the 1962 season when modifications to the 250GT's Colombo V12 engine upgraded it to full Testa Rossa specification....

THE ANCESTRY OF THE GTO

The first Ferrari 250 coupe was built for the 1952 running of the Mille Miglia road racing classic. From that time until the end of 1961 a dynasty of cars was established that would dominate competition in the Gran Turismo class. The GTO was the heir to this mighty tradition and would prove to be more than equal to the task of upholding it.

The Ferrari 250S of 1952 was a one-off based on the earlier 212 and 225 models. The installation of the 2953cc. Colombo V12 gave the car its 250 type number. With a few exceptions, this number would henceforth denote a Ferrari fitted with the short block engine. The engine in the original 250S had a 73mm. bore and 58.8mm. stroke. With three 36DCF Weber carburettors and a compression ratio of 8.2:1, 220b.h.p. was produced at 7000r.p.m.

A five-speed gearbox with a multi-plate clutch transmitted the power to the road. The tube frame chassis had a wheelbase of 2250mm. with a solid axle, semi-elliptical springs and Houdaille lever-type shock absorbers at the rear and wishbones and a single transverse leaf spring at the front. Each corner was equipped with drum brakes. The Vignale Berlinetta body was taken directly from the earlier, smaller engined 212 and 225.

Driven by Bracco and Rolfo, the 250S scored an heroic win on the Mille Miglia, defeating the might of the Mercedes Benz factory team. Further less glorious racing appearances resulted in retirements from Le Mans and the Carrera Pan Americana due to mechanical failures.

The Mille Miglia victory led to the development of the 250MM which was announced to the public at the Geneva Salon in 1953. Thirty-two examples were built on a chassis with the wheelbase lengthened to 2400mm. Fourteen examples had open Vignale Spider bodies, while the remainder were clothed in Pinin Farina Berlinetta panels.

The engine had undergone a major change resulting in individual intake ports finally replacing the twin port configuration of the original Colombo 125 unit. This improvement combined with new pistons, allowing the compression ratio to be raised to 9.0:1 brought about an increase in power to 240b.h.p. at 7200r.p.m. A four-speed, fully synchromesh gearbox replaced the 250S five-speed unit.

The 250MM failed on the 1953 Mille Miglia but won later in the year at Monza in the hands of Farina. Demonstrating the car's competitiveness even against prototype opposition, De Portago and Schell scored a remarkable second overall in the 1954 Buenos Aires 1000 kilometres.

1953 also saw the production of four open top cars designated the 250 Monza. These cars were based on a 2400mm. wheelbase ladder-type chassis, normally used to carry the large capacity four-cylinder Lampredi engine. This chassis was constructed from two large bore oval section main tubes cross-connected by thin diameter tubes to form a rigid base structure.

A De Dion tube was suspended at the rear of the Monza on a transverse leaf spring and lever-type shock absorbers. Wishbones and another transverse leaf were fitted at the front, although on the larger capacity 735 and 750 Monzas the front suspension was subsequently changed to coil springs. The Colombo V12 engine as used in the 250MM was fitted and in '53 the Monza won at Senigallia driven by Farina in front of Ferrari himself.

At the 1954 Paris Salon, Ferrari announced the 250 Europa, a stylish coupe built on a 2800mm. wheelbase chassis using similar suspension, brakes and transmission to the 250MM. The engine used, however, was the Lampredi-designed, fully square (68 x 68mm.) long block V12 which produced 200b.h.p. at 6000r.p.m. on three 36DCZ Weber carburettors.

Twenty-two of these road-going machines were built, of which eighteen received Pinin Farina's coupe-style body, one a Farina cabriolet body. The remaining three were clothed by Vignale in its coupe shell.

The 250 Europa is generally acknowledged as the forerunner of the Ferrari 250GT which first appeared in 1955. The 250GT chassis was evolved from the 250 Monza ladder frame with extra cross bracing in the centre and the wheelbase was increased to 2600mm. A solid rear axle was mounted on semi-elliptical leaf springs while the front suspension was by wishbones and coil springs. Those arrangements would remain unchanged throughout the various incarnations of the 250GT, including its most developed form, the GTO.

The transmission was via the four-speed unit as used on the Europa. Equipped with three of Weber's 36DCL or 36DCZ carburettors, the V12 engine produced 240b.h.p. at 7000r.p.m. Most of the early cars had a Farina coupe body evolved from the Europa shape, while a small number of Farina Berlinettas were produced for racing.

The racers featured aluminium bodywork and perspex side windows along with other weight-saving measures, which in conjunction with engine modifications resulted in a potent Gran Turismo competition car. The Le Mans disaster of 1955 prompted the introduction of an international GT series and Ferrari was ideally equipped to rule the roost. Such was the Ferrari domination of the 1956 Tour de France that the 250GT became known in some circles by that name.

Over succeeding years development of both the road-going and racing versions of the 250GT continued. Experiments with cold air ram induction in 1956 resulted in its introduction on all competition Berlinettas the following year. 1956 also saw the first use of lightweight aluminium bodies by Scaglietti for the racing versions. Subsequently, almost all the bodywork for the competition Berlinettas was produced by Scaglietti up to and beyond the GTO and the 250LM.

In 1957 a single plate Fichtel and Sachs clutch was fitted for the first time while in 1958 changes to engine block, timing case and sump contributed to an increase in power to 260b.h.p. These modifications, resulting from the Testa Rossa sports-racing car project, produced an engine designated the 128LM by the factory.

At the Paris Salon of 1959 a short wheelbase (2400mm.) version of the 250GT was introduced. This lightweight-bodied car had 280b.h.p. (at 7000r.p.m.) available from its 128F specification engine, which boasted a 9.2:1 compression ratio. The cars were also fitted with Dunlop disc brakes which had been introduced on the Testa Rossa sports racing machines earlier in the year.

The regular 250GT short wheelbase (s.w.b.) Berlinetta Competizione (or competition coupe) was virtually unbeatable at the dawn of the Sixties and won the Tour de France, the Tourist Trophy and Paris 1000 kilometres outright in addition to numerous class wins which resulted in a GT category victory in the 1960 Manufacturers' Championship. Ferrari domination continued in 1961 and the GT manufacturers' title went to Maranello again.

While customers were winning the marque another World Championship, the factory was busy preparing for the following season when there would be new regulations. The 1962 Manufacturers' Championship was to be contested solely by the GT categories. The championship was split into three divisions - up to 1000cc. (I), 1001-2000cc. (II) and over 2000cc. (III), with a World Title awarded to the winner of each. Even without taking into account a forthcoming new version of the 250GT, on existing form Ferrari looked a foregone winner of the biggest capacity title...

CHANGING SPORTS CAR RULES

A World Championship for Sportscars was announced in February 1953 at the CSI winter congress in Monaco, traditionally held during the Monte Carlo rally week. A seven-race series was proposed, including twenty-four races at Le Mans and Spa and two road racing classics, the Mille Miglia and the Carrera Pan Americana. The opening round at Sebring, Florida, was scheduled only five weeks after the announcement!

The races were to be a minimum of 1000 kilometres for cars complying to the FIA Appendix C of the International Sporting Code. This set of regulations, while specifying body dimensions, equipment to be fitted, and spare parts to be carried, put no restriction on engine size.

The first FIA World Sportscar Championship was won by Ferrari, victorious in three rounds of the series, from Jaguar which won at Le Mans. In 1954 Ferrari won the title again, beating Lancia by 12 points. However, Ferrari was beaten by two points in 1955, Mercedes-Benz victorious in a year marred by the disaster at Le Mans.

For 1956 the Automobile Club de l'Ouest imposed a 2.5 litre limit for Sports-Prototype cars and Le Mans was dropped from the championship. Ferrari won the title again, challenged only by Maserati, which won two rounds to the three of the Prancing Horse.

1957 saw the two Italian manufacturers stage a fierce battle for the championship which was only resolved at the final round in Venezuela where three works Maseratis were destroyed in separate incidents, giving the title to Ferrari again.

For 1958 an attempt was made to reduce maximum speeds by limiting engine capacity to no more than three litres. Maserati withdrew, having severe financial problems which had not been assisted by the carnage in South America. This left Ferrari with a clear run at the championship, which it won for the fifth time in six years. However, Aston Martin beat the red cars at the Nurburgring and Goodwood to take second place.

In 1959 Aston Martin upset the form book and won the world title after taking victories in the last three rounds of the championship, including Le Mans. Ferrari managed only a single win, in the opening round at Sebring.

At the end of the '59 season David Brown announced the withdrawal of the factory Aston Martin team, citing his disagreement with the regulations as a major reason: "I would like to see sports car racing where the cars are very closely allied to those the public can buy."

Enzo Ferrari expressed agreement, having earlier suggested the championship should be contested by Grand Turismo cars, which had been competing alongside the sports racing cars since the early years of the world series. For the 1960 season FIA regulation changes went part of the way to fulfilling Aston Martin and Ferrari wishes. Minimum windscreen height and luggage space requirements attempted to force participants to produce GT type cars, but several loopholes were left open and not surprisingly exploited.

Cars running in the specific GT class were required to be a model of which at least one hundred had been made in a period of twelve months, and were thus confined to mass produced bodies and engines of no more than three litres. Although the same engine capacity limit applied to sports racing and GT cars, there was no minimum production requirement for sports racers and thus no restriction on the type of engine used. Ferrari had a suitable purpose-built racing unit available, as did the returning Maserati team.

The screen height ruling became a major bone of contention during the 1960 season but there was a familiar result at the end of the five-race series. Ferrari tied with small capacity class ruler Porsche for the title on a best three performance rule but was adjudged the winner, having scored points in every round of the series, whereas the German manufacturer had failed to register in the final round at Le Mans.

By 1961 it seemed inevitable that the championship would be given over to GT cars but a further year's grace was given to the sports racing car. Ferrari triumphed yet again, beating Maserati by ten points.

At the CSI winter congress in Monaco in February 1961, the decision was finally taken to outlaw the sports racing car from the World Championship. It was proposed that from 1962 only GT cars complying with Appendix J of the International Sporting Code would be eligible for the World Manufacturers' Championship. Fuel capacity would be restricted according to engine size, with class divisions ranging from less than 1000cc. to over 3000cc. It appeared that the much talked of GT championship had been set in stone. However, the meeting was thrown into controversy by a request from the Italian representative for a GT prototype class.

The Le Mans organisers added further complication by announcing a class for Experimental cars with engines up to a 4.0 litre limit, fearing a small entry if their event was restricted solely to GT cars. Eventually a four-race series for Experimental cars was organised outside of the CSI under the banner of the Challenge Mondial de Vitesse, allowing points to be scored only by those manufacturers represented at every round. GT cars would also be eligible. Confusion reigned.

By its next meeting at the Monaco Grand Prix in May the CSI resolve had wavered and an announcement was made that the FIA would recognise the alternative series. It would be run alongside the GT series which would have three divisions, each subdivided into three classes and would comprise twelve rounds: nine in Europe and three in North America.

THE CREATION OF THE GTO

With the upgrading of Gran Turismo racing to Manufacturers' Championship status, Ferrari was eager to continue its dominance of the category. To this end a project to design and build a successor to the seemingly invincible 250GT SWB commenced towards the end of 1960. Under the direction of Ingenere Carlo Chiti, a group of engineers set out to create a car capable of winning Ferrari its eighth World Manufacturers' title in ten seasons. Franco Rocchi was to be responsible for the development of the engine, Giorgio Salvarini the gearbox and engineers Belli and Marchetti the chassis. Ingenere Giotto Bizzarini was to design the aerodynamic shape and to oversee testing and production.

The car was to be a further developed derivative of the SWB to abide by Appendix J and be eligible to run in the GT category. Chiti explains the design philosophy of the GTO thus: "All Ferrari GT cars were an evolution of the previous model and the GTO was an evolution of the 1960 short wheelbase Berlinetta. One of the main reasons for building the car was to try to make the V12 engine with Testa Rossa modifications more suitable for road use. Apart from the bodywork the GTO was not really an abrupt change from the SWB Berlinetta."

Ingenere Chiti recalls testing of GTO prototypes having commenced as early as March 1961 when Willy Mairesse ran a modified 250GT at Monza. "The car was used to test a modified version of the Testa Rossa type 168/61 engine in a GT chassis. Changes included larger valves, higher lift camshafts and higher compression pistons and new connecting rods."

The following month at the Le Mans test weekend in April 1961 a works Ferrari 250GT (chassis 2701GT) powered by the new specification engine was written off in a big accident by Jo Schlesser. The French driver, tired having driven overnight by road to the circuit, went off the track after the Dunlop

Le Mans 1961: the Tavano/Baghetti 250GT that was the forerunner of the GTO. This car - chassis 2643GT - broke its engine but at Daytona in '62 it finished fourth overall, winning Division III GT.

bridge, severely damaging the car and sustaining multiple fractures.

2701 had proved to be very fast earlier in the weekend when driven by Michael Parkes. The Englishman had attended the tests as part of the Rootes team to supervise the testing of a Sunbeam Alpine and had received an invitation from Ferrari team manager Romulo Tavoni to try one of the factory Berlinettas.

Parkes later recalled: "I was delighted with the chance and dressed in town kit, complete with tie and black shoes. I circulated round the long course as fast as I knew how. After half a dozen laps I rolled into the Ferrari pit, thanked them kindly and took myself off. Little did I realise that I had left a storm behind me. I had cut the Ferrari lap times by a considerable margin, earning a few well chosen and none too polite words from the works' drivers."

Thus began a special relationship between the tall, quietly spoken Parkes and the Maranello manufacturer that would last a decade. At the 1961 Le Mans race, Parkes was paired with Mairesse in a full-blown three-litre Testa Rossa sports racer. They finished second to the similar car of Olivier Gendebien and Phil Hill.

The factory also entered a 250GT SWB adorned with a Pininfarina-designed beaten aluminium body based on the Super America 400 road car and fitted with the dry sump type 168/61 engine running on six Weber 38DCN carburettors as tested in April. This GTO forerunner was entrusted to the current Ferrari boy wonder Giancarlo Baghetti, who was in the midst of sensationally winning his first three Formula One races, and Fernand Tavano, a French Ferrari enthusiast who had won the GT category in his own 250GT in the 1960 race.

During the early laps the car ran in the top ten but rain in the third hour dictated caution, which

GENESIS

Ing. Carlo Chiti

dropped the Franco-Italian crew to 13th place. As the weather improved 2643GT crept back up the lap charts to hold eighth place after nine hours. Three hours later a belch of smoke issuing from beneath the bonnet signalled an engine failure. The car was abandoned at Maison Blanche, leaving the driver with a relatively short walk back to the pits.

Subsequently, further testing was carried out using two more Berlinettas and the repaired Le Mans car. They were run at the Monza autodrome, the Modena airfield circuit and on the autostradas nearer the Maranello factory during the Summer of 1961. In July, Willy Mairesse carried out a long-distance test of 2053GT at Monza. This car had bodywork modifications in line with findings of tests in the wind tunnel at the Politecnico in Milan undertaken by project aerodynamicist Bizzarini. He was in attendance at Monza along with Chiti.

The engine was covered with a prototype front body panel that had been made in the factory body shop. This nose featured the classic triple nose duct configuration on its forward upper surface. Two of the ducts ram fed air via flexible hoses into a collector box containing the carburettor throats beneath a bulge in the bonnet panel. The rear of the car was standard 250GT, onto which had been added widened rear wheel arches and rear wing extensions. The same car was driven in further tests at Monza by Stirling Moss a few days prior to the Italian Grand Prix in September.

In November 1961 a dispute within the Ferrari competition department resulted in the departure of eight top executives including Bizzarini, Tavoni, Chief Engineer Chiti and production head Fausto Galarsi. After a short interval, two of the rebels reconsidered and received promotions on their return to Maranello. The remaining six (including the aforementioned quartet of big guns) decided to stick together and were recruited en masse by Automobili Turismo Sport Serenissima S.p.A.

This company had recently been formed by a trio of wealthy Italians; Count Giovanni Volpi di Misurata, a young aristocrat, Jaime Ortiz Patino, a businessman, and Giorgio Billi, an industrialist. Their intention was to produce racing and GT cars to compete with and beat Ferrari. Volpi's racing team Scuderia Serenissima Republicca di Venezia had run Ferrari GT cars since the late 1950s and had ordered

the first 250GTO off the production line to race in 1962 - before switching to the Chiti-designed A.T.S. GT car due to be ready for the 1963 season.

Having lost many of the key members of his team, Enzo Ferrari appointed a bespectacled young man by the name of Mauro Forghieri to the position of Chief Engineer at the age of 25. On his shoulders fell the responsibility of developing a variety of racing projects, including the fledgling 250GTO, to which project he had been contributing since its inception.

Despite this upheaval the first bona fide GTO (3223GT) was ready before the end of the year and was shaken down by Mairesse at Modena on 3rd December 1961.

At the end of February 1962 Ferrari held its annual press conference. At this event the reigning Formula One World Champion Constructor and Sportscar World Manufacturers' Champion announced the revised Chiti-designed shark-nose Grand Prix and sports racing cars. Also on display was its new contender for GT honours, chassis 3223GT, looking resplendent in traditional scarlet with a patriotic longitudinal stripe of red, white and green.

The GTO looked far more aerodynamic than its GT predecessors and was evidently a purposeful racing machine from the tip of its elongated streamlined nose to the end of its sharply cut off Kamm tail. Unlike the sports racing cars it was shown alongside, it did not carry a new-fangled rear spoiler, an omission that would soon be rectified as testing commenced.

American driver Ritchie Ginther is credited with introducing the aerodynamic spoiler as a cure for the high-speed body-lifting tendencies of the Ferrari Dino sports racing car at a test session in 1961. After experiments with a longitudinal fin proved inconclusive the American, drawing on his previous aircraft experience, suggested that a piece of aluminium sheet should be riveted across the trailing edge of the car's tail. The improvement in handling was so dramatic that within a short space of time the spoiler came into widespread use on competition and eventually road cars.

The first two examples of the GTO received riveted aluminium sheet spoilers and from the third car onward the aerodynamic device was an integral part of the rear body panel.

The 250GT's original 2600mm. wheelbase had been

reduced to 2400mm. on the SWB chassis homologated during the 1960 season and this dimension was carried over to the GTO. Similarly, the GTO retained the SWB's all round disc brakes and its independent front suspension. At the rear the car still relied upon an outdated leaf spring arrangement.

This compromise was one that Ferrari felt constrained to accept, given that the new car had to be accepted as a development of the SWB. In wishing to race what was in effect a Testa Rossa-engined 250GT in 1962 without the bother of constructing the 100 examples required for GT homologation, Ferrari felt it should stick with the old rear suspension.

The GTO took the inevitable class win on its debut at Sebring in March 1962. Production at the factory was in full swing by April, the win in Florida made the potential obvious and a long queue of eager customers quickly formed.

Ing. Mauro Forghieri(in hat) with Dragoni.

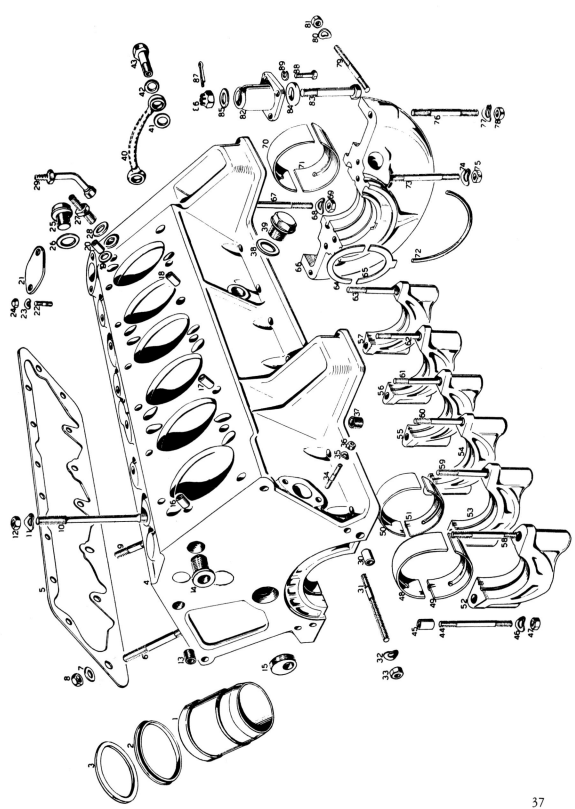

250 GTO TECHNICALITIES

The heart of the Ferrari 250 GTO was its Tipo 168/62 engine. This was a water-cooled 60 degree V12 of 2953cc. Testa Rossa blocks were fitted in the first two cars produced but were replaced in subsequent examples by the 128E Silumin blocks first produced in 1960 for the SWB. Cast iron liners with an internal diameter of 73.0mm. were forced into the bottom of the block. The bores were swept to a stroke length of 58.8mm. by light alloy Borgo pistons with two compression rings and one oil control ring.

Fully floating gudgeon pins attached the pistons to the forged connecting rods which had phosphor bronze self-lubricating small end bushes and Vandervell thinwall big end bearings. Castellated big end bolts with split pins were initially fitted but were later replaced with self-locking bolts. The steel crankshaft machined from a solid billet was mounted in seven Vandervell thinwall plain main bearings. The twenty-litre alloy dry sump contained scavenge and feeder pumps.

Separate Testa Rossa cylinder heads housed a single overhead camshaft per bank driven by a triple row timing chain, itself powered by a spur gear and reduction sprocket from the crankshaft nose. Phosphor bronze shrunk-in valve seats contained a single exhaust and a single intake (non sodium) valve per cylinder sprung by double coils in unsealed aluminium and copper guides. The water pump was driven by the timing chain.

The fuel mixture was regulated by six Weber 38 DCN double choke carburettors. Initially cold air ram induction via ducting on the nose was used but all cars subsequently ran with warm air, non-pressurised systems.

A 14mm. Marchal 34 HF or 33 R spark plug per cylinder was mounted outside the vee above the exhaust primaries. The plugs were fired by twin Marelli distributors with two coils and two condensers. The 12 volt battery was charged by a 300 watt dynamo-type generator belt driven from a shaft powered by timing chain. The electrical system also operated two Bendix Bluetop fuel pumps.

The compression ratio was set at 9.5:1 and 296 - 302 b.h.p. was produced at 7500 r.p.m. with torque quoted as 35 kg./m. at 5000 r.p.m. The factory recommended maximum r.p.m. was 8000 but many engines were taken beyond this without drastic consequences and it was not unusual for the tell-tale to show 8500 - 8600 r.p.m. after a race.

The exhaust system comprised two three-into-one primaries on each side of the engine feeding into one silencer box per bank. Twin pipes from the rear of the silencer merged into single, large-bore tubes which divided again into pairs with a Snap exhaust extractor at the tail of each pipe.

The fuel consumption at Le Mans was calculated as 37 litres per 100 kilometres.

A single dry plate Fichtel and Sachs clutch coupled the engine to the transmission. A new Ferrari designed five-speed gearbox was employed, this having Porsche patented baulk ring synchromesh and its own separate oil pump. The rear axle carried a ZF patented self-locking limited slip differential made under licence by Ferrari. Crown wheel and pinion ratios ranged from 4.85:1 to 3.55:1.

The GTO chassis was a steel, ladder-type frame as first used in the 1954 250 Monza. Two main tubes were cross-braced and reinforced with triangulated sections beneath the doors and with upper framework to support the body panels. The engine was secured within the frame ahead of the cockpit area on four mounting points.

The front suspension was by parallel forged double wishbones with (non-adjustable) helical springs mounted between the wishbones and a lighter co-axial helical spring and Koni damper unit mounted above. An anti-roll bar was employed. Steering was by a ZF worm and peg system.

At the rear a live axle was mounted on semi-elliptical leaf springs interleaved with rubber strips. Koni dampers were also fitted, offering the facility to utilise compensating co-axial helical springs. Two torque arms on each side connected the chassis frame and axle tube, which was laterally located by a Watts linkage mounted on the differential casing and connected via tubes to the chassis.

Braking was by outboard mounted cast iron Dunlop discs with Dunlop single pot calipers of light alloy or cast iron. Two- and one-eighth-inch diameter pistons were used at the front, one-and-three-quarter-inch at rear. Ferodo DS11 pads were listed as standard.

Steel half shafts with Rudge Whitworth 42mm. steel hubs and three-eared knock-off caps carried Borrani wire wheels with steel spokes and duraluminium rims of 6" x 15" at the front and 6.5" x 15" at the rear, shod with Dunlop R5/R6 racing tyres, 600L x 15 front, 700L x 15 rear.

At the rear was a 29.5 gallon (133 litre) hand riveted double-skinned aluminium fuel tank and a 4.5 gallon (200 litre) oil tank. Water and oil radiators were mounted in the nose.

The hand-beaten aluminium two-door coupe body was by Carozzeria Scaglietti to a design by Giotto Bizzarini. A Triplex laminated glass windscreen was fitted with plexiglass side and rear windows.

At the Le Mans test weekend a number of eyebrows would be raised by the appearance of a GTO chassis with the 4.0 litre SuperAmerica engine in place of the familiar 3.0 litre unit. The 77mm. x 71mm. 3967cc. V12 was equipped with three Weber 46DCF3 carburettors and produced 340b.h.p. at 6,750r.p.m. A non-synchromesh four speed transmission was used and the tube frame chassis and the body were pure GTO aside from a pronounced bulge in the bonnet panel made necessary by the taller block of the engine.

It was in this guise that the 4.0 litre GTO would race at the 'Ring as a Prototype. By the time of the '62 Le Mans race the size of the bonnet bulge would be higher bearing testimony to the fitting of six 42DCN carburettors between the cylinder banks, this increasing power to 390b.h.p. at 7,500r.p.m.

GTO DIMENSIONS

2400mm. 93.6" wheelbase
1351mm. 152.8" front track
1346mm. 152.4" rear track
Overall length 4400mm. 171.6"
Overall height 1245mm. 48.5"
Dry weight 2300 - 2400lbs.

The 330LMB was a sister to the GTO and this example driven by Sears/Salmon finished sixth at Le Mans in 1963. Run by Maranello, the car enjoyed a careful outing.

Corrado Ferlaino - later Presdient of the Napoli Football Club - ran his GTO on the '64 Targa Florio. Rebodied at the end of '63, the car finished fifth, first GT home.

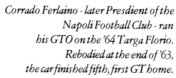

The light blue rear panel of Michael Salmon's GTO picks it out from this mixed bag of runners in the '65 Nurburgring 1000Kms. Note the Ferrari 250LM among its rivals.

Bulgari/Grana finished fourth overall and first GT on the '63 Targa Florio. The car was GTO 3413, owned by Bulgari and entered by the Scuderia Centro Sud.

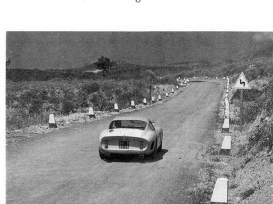

At Le Mans in 1965 the Cobra steam roller was stopped in its tracks by a rush of engine and clutch failures. This Ferrari 275 GTB, the succesor to the GTO, entered by Ecurie Francorchamps and driven by Willy Mairesse Berelys' won the big GT catergory finishing a fine third overall.

1962

INTRODUCTION

In its first season, the Championnat International des Constructeurs Grand Tourisme for cars complying to Appendix J would be contested over a series of nine races for the largest capacity cars, those in Division III (over 2000cc). Twelve races had originally been planned but the seemingly inevitable cancellations occurred. Parallel Championships were held for Divisions I and II, the Divisions running together at some events but not all.

Each Division would be sub-divided into two classes in the race results but points would be awarded on the basis of 9-6-4-3-2-1 regardless of class sub-division. Only the best five scores of a manufacturer counted towards its Championship points tally.

1962 GT Championship, Division III

11.02.62	Intercontinental 3 Hours, Daytona USA
24.03.62	12 Hours of Sebring USA
06.05.62	Targa Florio, Piccolo Madonie, Sicily I
27.05.62	ADAC 1000Kms., Nurburgring D
23.06.62	
24.06.62	24 Heures du Mans, Le Mans F
15.07.62	Auvergne Trophy, La Charade F
18.08.62	Tourist Trophy, Goodwood GB
08.09.62	Double 500, Bridgehampton USA
21.10.62	Paris 1000Kms., Montlhery F

Le Mans 1962: the GTO forerunner - 2643GT - was out again, this time driven by Hugus/Reed who finished ninth overall. Since the '61 race it had been sold to NART and at Daytona had been driven by Stirling Moss.

The Challenge Mondial de Vitesse des Prototypes Grand Tourisme would comprise four rounds: Sebring, the Targa Florio, the 'Ring and Le Mans. In Britain a national championship for GT and sports-racing cars was sponsored and organised by Autosport magazine. The best five performances in class at selected races qualified cars for a three hour race into darkness at Snetterton at the end of the season.

GTO RIVALS

Brands Hatch 1962: Carlo Mario Abate in the Breadvan. Unable to purchase a GTO early in the '62 season, Count Volpihad rush-produced this highly modified 250GT with very creative aerodynamics.

Following a long run of competition success with the D Type that included three wins at Le Mans, Jaguar's new E Type Sports car was eagerly anticipated. When it was finally unveiled in the spring of 1961 a four-year wait proved to have been worthwhile. Derived from the D Type and bristling with innovation, the E Type's announcement was nothing short of sensational.

A familiar 3781cc. (87mm. x 106mm.) straight six twin overhead camshaft engine fitted with three SU carburettors offered a substantial 265b.h.p. at 5,500r.p.m. It was mounted in a tubular steel sub frame attached to a monocoque-type centre section constructed from a number of 20 gauge pressed steel sections welded together to form a rigid structure. The D Type's front suspension of wishbones and torsion bars was also mounted on the subframe while

at the rear another subframe carried a new independent suspension system. There were combined coil spring and damper units, trailing links, lower arms and an anti roll bar while the drive shafts formed the upper arms.

Jaguar had pioneered the use of disc brakes in racing but it was still a surprise to find them fitted on a road car. The front pair were 11" in diameter and were mounted outboard while the rears were 10" diameter and were mounted inboard, either side of the differential. The transmission was by the XK150S four speed gearbox with synchromesh above first gear and mated to the engine by a single plate dry clutch. All this machinery was clothed in a steel body, with echoes of the D Type and designed by the same airflow expert: Malcolm Sayer. In road trim the car weighed in at 2688lbs.

No plans were made by the factory to race the car but in 1961 a number of privately entered E Types began to appear on the tracks. Many competition cars were lightened by their owners and some met with success in British sprint races driven by Graham Hill, Roy Salvadori and Dick Protheroe among others.

While the E Type was the only serious threat to the GTO from a rival marque in '62, Ferrari also faced competition from a much modified 250GT. Due to bad blood between Ferrari and the Scuderia Serenissima Republica de Venezia over the SSR's employment of the Ferrari defectors, Count Volpi found his orders for the first two GTOs off the production line cancelled by Enzo Ferrari personally. In view of that, defector Bizzarini resolved to create an even better car from the 250GT, based on his working knowledge of the GTO project.

Over a surprisingly short period of time a number of major changes were made to an ex-Gendebien 250GT SWB. This car was raced in original guise for the last time at Sebring in March '62, then the SSR got to work.

The improvements devised by Bizzarini were carried out by Neri and Bonaccini. They included lowering the engine by conversion to a dry sump while power was enhanced via the installation of six Weber 38DCN carburettors. The engine was then mounted far back in the chassis to improve the weight distribution, the wheelbase remaining at 2400mm. The intention was to race the car as an improved SWB model. The five speed gearbox of the GTO was unavailable so the standard four speed unit had to be employed.

The most striking feature of the car was its beaten aluminium body. This began with an aggressively pointed nose perforated with two squared off nostrils in its upper surface and a single inlet beneath which fed the water and oil radiators. The headlights were under streamlined perspex covers mounted at the front of wheel arches that rose either side of a gently curved bonnet panel. The induction stacks, domed with perspex, protruded through the bonnet, ahead of a windscreen retained from the SWB.

The roofline sloped infinitesimally rearward until it terminated abruptly, as per the theories of Doctor Kamm, in an upright panel which was dominated by a flat rear window. The rear wheel arches were flared upward and aft in a similar manner making a curious stepped outline when viewed from the rear. The car's distinctive lines earned it the nickname of 'Breadvan'.

Silverstone International Trophy meeting 1963: Graham Hill's E Type Jaguar leads Michael Parkes' GTO. The Jaguar was a key rival for the GTO in '62 and '63 but lacked direct factory support.

GTO RACE RECORD

Due to a delay in homologation the 250GTO was ineligible to participate in the first round of the GT championship, the three-hour race at Daytona, Florida, on February 11th. However, the 1961 Le Mans special had been sold during the winter to the North American Racing Team run by Ferrari stalwart Luigi Chinetti. For the Daytona race the Le Mans car was lent to the UDT-Laystall team to be driven by its Formula One driver Stirling Moss. The race was won by 1961 Formula One World Champion Phil Hill and multiple Le Mans winner Olivier Gendebien in a Testa Rossa, while Moss took fourth place overall and won the big GT class, opening Ferrari's 1962 Championship campaign with a maximum score.

The GTO made its competition debut at the Sebring 12 hours, the second GT round and the first race in the Challenge Mondial de Vitesse. Chassis 3387GT, the second car completed, was driven by Gendebien/Hill and finished second overall, winning the GT class. The NART-entered car was, however, out-run in the early stages by SSR de Venezia's 250GT driven by Davis/Tavano until it retired with broken gearbox.

At the Le Mans test weekend in April the Ferrari team arrived late, having had to divert to avoid snow at the French border. It missed the whole Saturday practice session. On the Sunday the fastest times were set by Ferrari's secret weapon, a 4.0 litre GTO (3763SA) which was driven by Parkes, Mairesse and Bandini. The Belgian driver also completed a number of laps in the first customer 250 GTO: 3505GT, eventually destined for the UDT Laystall Team for Moss to drive.

The GTO made its British racing debut at the Easter Monday BARC Goodwood International Trophy meeting. Two examples were entered for the 15-lap Sussex Trophy race for Sports and GT cars that closed the day's proceedings. These were the UDT

Targa Florio 1962: the Ferraro/Scarlatti GTO. This was the European debut for the new GT contender and it finished fourth overall, winning Division III GT. The same car is seen in its pits on pages 8 - 9.

car for Innes Ireland and 3589GT entered by British Ferrari importers Maranello Concessionaires and Tommy Sopwith's Equipe Endeavour for Parkes. The cars were driven across country from the Ferrari factory at Maranello to the channel and arrived in England the night before the meeting.

The UDT car was withdrawn after the accident that befell Moss in the Formula One event earlier in the afternoon, Ireland switching to UDT's Lotus 19 sports-racer that Moss had been down to drive. The race was duly won by Ireland with Parkes second overall, winning the GT class.

Round two of the Challenge Mondial de Vitesse was the Targa Florio held in Sicily on the 6th May. The works GTO of Giorgio Scarlatti/Paulo Ferraro - 3451GT - finished fourth overall behind two Ferrari sports racers and a Porsche prototype, winning the GT class.

Both British-based GTOs took part in the GT race at the Silverstone International Trophy Meeting in May. Parkes was in the Maranello/Endeavour car, Masten Gregory in the unraced UDT machine. The GTOs finished 1-2 in the race, ahead of Graham Hill in John Coombs' E Type Jaguar and Jim Clark in the Aston Martin DB4GT Zagato entered by the Essex Racing Team. The Ferraris both set laps at an average speed of over 100m.p.h., the first time GT cars had achieved such a feat at Silverstone.

The 4.0 litre GTO made its race debut at the A.D.A.C. 1000 kilometres on the daunting Nurburgring north circuit. Entered by the factory in the Experimental class, 3763SA was driven by Parkes/Mairesse. The car was second fastest in practice behind Hill/Gendebien in a 246SP sports racer. Scarlatti/Ferraro were fastest in the GT class in 3451.

The 4.0 litre led briefly after the retirement of Clark's Lotus 23, until its routine stop for fuel at which

*Le Mans 1962: Elde/
Beurlys lead the 4.0
litre GTO of
Parkes/ Bandini
which retired with
overheating. The
Belgians finished
fourth overall. The
sister GTO of
Guichet/Noblet
pictured on page 12
finished second.*

Mairesse handed over to Parkes. Parkes then traded the lead with Hill until the prototype moved clear in the last quarter of the race. Gunther Kochert/ Umberto Maglioli in GTO 3527GT led the GT class for the first 14 laps until the starter motor failed at a pitstop. Scarlatti/Ferraro crashed and Ferrari were rescued by German privateers Nocker/Seidel in a 250GT, taking the class win from the similar car of Noblet/Guichet.

The Mallory Park 2000 Guineas meeting saw the debut of a second Maranello-owned car entered by Bowmaker for John Surtees (3647), alongside Parkes in his regular GTO. Parkes won easily from Hill's E Type with Surtees less than half a second behind at the finish.

At the final round of the Challenge Mondial Vitesse, the Le Mans twenty-four hours, there were six genuine GTOs entered along with the 1961 GTO prototype (2643), the 4.0 litre GTO (3765SA) and Scuderia Serenissima's outrageous Breadvan (2819).

The 4.0 litre car was second fastest in practice in the hands of Parkes/Bandini and was close to the front of the start line-up, since the cars were assembled in order according to engine capacity. Graham Hill got the Project 212 Aston Martin moving first and led the field away. Parkes held second until he spun off into a sandbank at the end of the Mulsanne straight.

The GTOs were led at the end of the first lap by Jean Guichet/Pierre Noblet in Guichet's own car - 3705GT - from Fernand Tavano/Andre Simon in Tavano's 3769GT, Vaccarella/Scarlatti in the 3445GT of Scuderia Serenissima and Bob Grossman and NASCAR Star Glenn "Fireball" Roberts in NART's 33887GT. All were well up the order, mixing it with Ferrari and Maserati Experimentals driven by the likes of Pedro Rodriguez and Bruce McLaren.

Parkes managed to dig 3765SA out of the sand but overheating caused by accident damage put the car out in the fifth hour. Meanwhile, the Breadvan led the GTOs but it lasted only just over two hours before transmission failure sidelined it. The car had been rush-built, its prop shaft had not been properly balanced and had broken...

Tavano/Simon were sixth after five hours and ran consistently in the top six until the differential bearings broke up just after 7.00a.m. on Sunday. Ireland/ Gregory in the UDT car climbed to seventh by midnight, only to lose two laps having the dynamo replaced, further electrical problems causing retirement in the 14th hour.

Scarlatti/Vaccarella reached the top ten during the night, then they too had differential trouble which, combined with valve damage, put them out of the race as dawn broke.

At the finish Noblet/Guichet were second overall, while the Ecurie Francorchamps 3757GT of Elde/Beurlys was fourth. Grossman/Roberts were sixth overall but, for some obscure reason, their GTO had been entered in the Experimental class. Hugus and Reed in 2643 took ninth overall and fourth in the big GT division behind the Cunningham/Salvadori E Type Jaguar.

The sixth round of the GT series was held on the tortuous La Charade Circuit near Clermont Ferrand in mid July. The 190-mile Auvergne Trophy was poorly supported and was won by Carlo Maria Abate in the Scuderia Serenissima car 3446GT, Guichet in 3705 was fourth behind Simons' 250GT.

In England the Scott Brown Trophy at Snetterton saw Parkes and Surtees in their regular GTOs finish second and third, beaten by Graham Hill's Lotus 19.

The August Bank Holiday meeting at Brands Hatch featured the 25-lap Peco Trophy for which six GTOs were entered, Parkes and Surtees in the Maranello cars, Ireland in UDT's 3505, Colin Davis in SSR's 3445 plus two new cars: Roy Salvadori in John Coombs' 3729 and David Piper in his own car, 3767, a new chassis which had been driven by road from Modena.

Parkes was delayed at the start, having had the plugs changed after the warm-up lap, Surtees led initially from his teammate with Salvadori third in the white car, chased by Ireland in the light green car, Piper's green example, Hill's E Type and Davis. Parkes took the lead on the second lap and, despite rain, led for the remainder of the race.

Surtees held second until he spun in the wet, letting Salvadori and Ireland through. Davis badly damaged Count Volpi's car when a front brake locked and he hit the bank at Druids. Salvadori finished second with Surtees recovering to finish third, 1.8 seconds ahead of Ireland, with Hill narrowly ahead of Piper in fifth. In the Guards Trophy race at the same meeting, Abate took fourth place in the Bread-

van, having led Bonnier's SSR Testa Rossa for 30 of the 50 laps in a race won by Parkes in a 246SP.

The GT championship continued with the Tourist Trophy at Goodwood on 18th August. The five British-based GTOs were entered as per the Peco Trophy, aside from Hill replacing Salvadori in the Coombs car. After practice Ireland, Surtees, Parkes, Hill, Salvadori in an E Type and Piper headed the line-up for the Le Mans start.

Ireland led the first two laps until passed by Surtees. Hill was third ahead of Clark's Aston Martin, followed by Piper and Salvadori. Parkes' engine misfired at the start, dropping him to midfield on the first lap, but he recovered to 10th on lap two as the engine cleared. At the twenty-five lap - quarter distance - mark, four GTOs were at the head of the field, Surtees leading Ireland, Parkes (continuing his recovery) and Hill.

At half-distance, after fuel stops Surtees still led from Ireland, Hill, Salvadori, Parkes, Clark's Aston Martin and Piper. Surtees pressed on and broke the GT lap record while Parkes had a moment avoiding Kerrison's spinning 250GT. Surtees looked set to win until he came up to lap Clark for the second time on lap 63. The Aston spun, moving over to let the Ferrari through. Both cars collided, hit the earth bank at Madgwick and were too badly damaged to continue. Ireland took the lead and was 20 seconds ahead of Parkes at three-quarter distance. Following at a similar interval was Hill from Salvadori, Piper and Kerrison.

Parkes spun trying to catch Ireland and lost second to Hill, falling behind by half a minute. Robin Benson, who had taken over the Kerrison 250GT, lost control at Madgwick and added further damage to the cars of Surtees and Clark. Hill had closed the gap to four seconds by the finish, despite a windscreen smeared with oil from a cracked ignition coil. However, Ireland ran out the winner with Parkes third ahead of Salvadori and Piper.

Ireland was lucky not to incur the usual 60-second penalty for short-cutting the chicane. The observer who reported the early race indiscretion by the brake snatch afflicted UDT Laystall car said he felt Ireland's emergency manoeuvre to have been justified. So Ferrari came away with a clean sweep of the top three places.

For the 5000 kilometre Tour de France, eight

Tour de France 1962, two hour race at Le Mans: the Schlesser/Oreiller GTO is dug out of the Mulsanne corner sand. On pages 5 - 6 this car is seen at the start, beaten off the line by the GTO of Abate/Bettoja.

Tour de France 1962. A scene at a rest halt during the course of the long, gruelling rally cum race. Car 151 is the GTO of Bianchi/Dubois while car 157 is the similar machine of Tavano/Martin.

only for Abate to become involved in an accident with Guichet in the race at the Charade circuit. Abate was forced to retire soon afterwards when his co-driver fell ill. Guichet's tour ended when he collided with a lorry in the Pyrenees, heavily damaging his car and injuring his co-driver, who was hurled against the windscreen.

The demise of Abate put Berney/Gretener into the lead until they suffered a broken half shaft, which promoted Bianchi/Dubois to the head of the field. Driving carefully, the Belgian pair held onto the lead by consistent finishing - it was only towards the end of the event that they finally took a stage win, when Bianchi set the fastest time at Mont Revard.

With just the two-hour races at Spa and Rheims remaining, the Belgians looked a good bet for victory. After taking a steady third place at Spa they began the untimed road section to Rheims with seemingly a winning lead. Alas, just before the border their car was in collision with a milk truck and the front bodywork was severely damaged.

Under the direction of Gaetano Florini from the Ferrari factory, the bent nose panels were removed, the chassis was straightened as best it could be and a bonnet panel was fashioned from a sheet of aluminium. Sadly the car was rejected by the scrutineers at Rheims because of the damage and a lack of lights, so it was unable to complete the final stage. Despite this, the Belgians' points total placed them seventh overall.

Of the others, Tavano and Martin were sidelined with engine trouble. Darville and Langlois van Ophem took third overall after a steady run, while Piper and Margulies were classified fifth on the gruelling event, having looked set for a higher placing until they incurred penalties for arriving late at a control.

Second place fell to Schlesser/Oreiller, who spent the whole tour making up time lost by Schlesser when he buried the car in the notorious sandbank at Le Mans in the early days of the event. Hill climb specialist Oreiller set best times on a number of stages, but was unable to regain enough time to threaten the winning 250GT of Simon and Duprey.

The British racing season ended with the Autosport Three Hours at Snetterton. Parkes in 3589 won the race, having driven the freshly overhauled car from the Ferrari factory to the Norfolk circuit, arriving at 1.00a.m. on race morning. The Maranello

GTOs were entered. Lucien Bianchi and Claude Dubois were in 3527, an ex-works car bought by Bianchi and entered by Ecurie Francorchamps. Abate and Bettoja were in SSR's 3445, Guichet and Clement were in Guichet's 3705, Darville and Gerald Langlois van Ophem were in 3757 owned by Leon Dernier and entered by Ecurie Francorchamps. Piper and Margulies were in Piper's 3767 - repaired after its owners' indiscretion at a Crystal Palace club meeting - Tavano and Martin were in Tavanos' 3769, Oreiller and Schlesser were in Schlesser's 3851 and Berney and Gretener were in Berney's 3909. The car was entered by Scuderia Filipinetti and was running in its first event since acquired from the factory.

Abate/Bettoja led the GT category at half-distance,

car was involved in a battle for the lead with Clark's Lotus 23, which was recovering from an early delay with a jammed gearbox and a spin on fuel leaking from its own tank.

The Lotus took the lead as dusk fell only to lose it as the gearbox malfunctioned again, leaving Parkes an unchallenged win. Piper in 3767 also raced but, due to confusion in the dark with lap charts and time-keepers, it is difficult to know what happened to this car, apart from a spin at Coram Curve as captured by Autosport photographer George Phillips!

The penultimate round of the GT Championship came at Bridgehampton with the Double 500 meeting on 15-16 September. The entry was poor, not a single European attending despite the race's World Championship status. Grossman finished second overall and first GT in 3387 ahead of Ed Hugus and George Reed in NART's 3223.

The Coupe du Salon held at Montlhery in honour of the Paris Motor Show was the scene of the only competition fatality in a GTO. The promising French driver Henri Oreiller in his own car 3851 left his seat belt off to gain time in the Le Mans-type start, crashed and was impaled on the gear lever. Berney/Gretener took a devalued win in 3909 with Dernier third in 3757.

The GT Championship finale, the Paris 1000Kms. at the same circuit on 21st October, was graced by eight GTOs and the Breadvan. Vaccarella/Abate drove SSR's 3445, Surtees/Parkes Maranello's 3647, rebuilt after its TT accident (marking the team's first race abroad), Mairesse/Bianchi 3527, rebuilt after its Tour de France mauling. Beurlys (the pseudonym behind which Jean Blaton raced)/Langlois van Ophem drove the second Ecurie Francorchamps car, Swiss Kalman Von Csazy/Hubert, the former's 3809, taking part in its first International event, having run in minor German races previously. Berney/Bordeu drove 3909, entered on this occasion by SSR, Guichet/Noblet 3943 - Noblet's new car - while a new car was entered by NART for Pedro and Riccardo Rodriguez: 3987. The Breadvan was entrusted to Davis and Scarfiotti.

The Rodriguez brothers took an easy win, only losing the lead during the first fuel stop. Behind them the Maranello car came home in second place, overcoming a misfire, an oil leak and controversial one-minute penalty for putting a wheel over a painted line marking the correct entry to the pits.

Next up was the Breadvan, which had fought off the challenges from Guichet/Noblet and Mairesse/Bianchi. Vaccarella/Abate went out with a broken differential, having been as high as third. Berney/Bordeu retired with engine failure, having run in the top six, and were classified 22nd at the finish. Von Csazy crashed 3809 heavily enough to prevent him continuing, while the other Francorchamps car, 3757, was disqualified when "Remordu" (Guy Ancez) took the car out onto the track, the regulations not allowing three drivers.

At the end of the European season David Piper took his car to South Africa to contest the Rand Nine Hours at Kyalami. Piper shared the car with Bruce Johnstone from Durban, whom he had met during his time racing in Formula One. The GTO won the race, which was run in unseasonably foul weather. A problem arose when the car's spare wheels were lost in transit and the team had to borrow the wheels from the local Ferrari importer's road car. Despite the wheels not being a perfect fit and a challenge from a local Lotus 23, the GTO won by a lap. Piper then finished third in the Angola Grand Prix, in 3767.

The year ended with the traditional Speed Week in the Bahamas. At the Nassau Tourist Trophy Roger Penske in 3987GT sold to John Mecom by NART was first ahead of Bandini/Hayes in NART 3223GT and Ireland in 3589, now owned by Tom O'Connor's Rosebud Team of Victoria Texas. In later events, Charlie Hayes took 3223 to third place in the Nassau Governors' Trophy and fifth in the Nassau Trophy.

Ferrari's domination of Division III was complete. Without running a works programme it had won every round of the series and had scored maximum points. Even when the GTOs failed, as the the 'Ring, there had been those SWBs on hand to save the Prancing Horse. Jaguar took second place in the Championship thanks to the efforts of its customers while Chevrolet's third place in the series came from points scored in the American rounds only. Ferrari scored 45 points, Jaguar 16 and Chevrolet nine, while Lancia notched up four points, Aston Martin only one.

The GT Prototype series also resulted in a maximum score for Ferrari after victories at each round. With its smaller capacity car Porsche took second place having been the only other manufacturer to contest all events.

BEHIND THE WHEEL

Phill Hill

Oliver Gendebien

Innes Ireland

PHIL HILL
Sebring 12 hours

"I was annoyed at being put in the GTO. I wanted to be in one of the proper prototypes. To me the car that would finish first, regardless of which cars could score in the championship was the one that mattered. It was like racing for the Index of Performance at Le Mans, you can keep it ...

"I felt that we were being discriminated against because I wouldn't sign a contract for 1962. I had been considering other things, I had talked to BRM, I had been in big arguments and I'd heard the rumours that the whole bunch at Maranello were walking out and going to Bologna to start another company. Ferrari had tried to force me into signing a contract but I knew that any time they were that anxious about me signing, there must be something wrong.

"So I resisted but I didn't know why. So I felt that this was the tail end of what had gone on earlier, at the end of 1961 and that it was reason why we got stuck in a GTO gran turismo car instead of the proper prototype with a chance for an overall win.

"It was a very nice car, except I didn't like the gearbox. It was heavy and slow, with big Porsche synchromesh cones and baulking rings and the shift was way up here. Everything else I had driven for them was a nice little snatch change with no synchros and lightweight gears but this was for the klutzy driver that needed to have the gears synchronised and I didn't like it at all.

"In the race I remember that the elapsed time from going into the Hangar Straightaway to the Webster Z turns was so little different between the GTO and the Prototype, there was hardly anything in it. The GTO got out of the hairpin turns so well that it took the prototype all kinds of late braking to get by us. So from that point of view it was very novel

and I found myself wondering why we weren't using this engine in the prototypes."

OLIVIER GENDEBIEN
Sebring 12 hours

"I think the reason we were given a gran turismo car at Sebring was because the 1962 World Championship was in GT. For me I don't believe it was anything to do with contracts. I hadn't signed a contract with Ferrari since 1959. That year I said to him, 'The contract is a one way contract. You don't pay me enough money to buy cigarettes but I don't smoke so I don't care but I'm happy to drive Ferraris. So I don't want to sign any more contracts with you. You have very good cars and if you want me to drive for you I would be very pleased but without a contract'. So I still raced for Ferrari at Le Mans.

"It was memorable for me because it was my third win at Sebring, although we finished behind a Testa Rossa we were first for the World Championship."

INNES IRELAND
Sussex Trophy, Goodwood

"Ronnie Hoare and I went out to collect the cars. We swapped the   cars about coming back but I had gone out to the Ferrari factory to collect the UDT Laystall car and Ronnie had gone out for his. Only one GTO had left the factory before that, so ours were the second and third cars which we took delivery of on the same day.

"We drove them up to the north coast of France, put them on the Silver City cross channel air ferry and flew them into Southampton, got them off the plane and went straight to Goodwood. After a change of plugs and wheels I was practising with my car, an hour after getting to the circuit. Ronnie Hoare had Mike Parkes driving his car.

"I was down to drive the Ferrari in the combined Sports and GT race and Stirling was going to drive the Lotus 19. But after his accident the team scratched the Ferrari and I drove the Lotus for which I had been nominated as second driver. Stirling never actually practiced with the GTO as far as I recall. It was obvious that the winning car was going to be the Lotus and Stirling was never one to want to come second."

JOHN MINNEY
Sussex Trophy, Goodwood

"I can remember Ron Chubb and I having been over the pub, coming back to the workshop at F. English in Bournemouth waiting for the cars to arrive. They arrived later than we expected, I don't think they were driven into the workshop until about half past ten at night.

"We'd already had a lot of experience with the 250GT and although the GTO was a new car it had a similar engine, transmission and rear axle layout. Apart from the new body and dashboard it was really just an update of a well proven car. We had very little to do to it. I'm not sure that we even changed the oil. We listened to what Ronnie Hoare and Innes had to say about the way the car drove but I don't think there were any particular jobs to do on the cars that night. We just did a spanner check, checked fluid levels and then loaded them up and took them to Goodwood."

MINNEY
Silverstone International Trophy, GT race

"Obviously there were a lot of people at that meeting at Silverstone. We were all absolutely over the moon about Michael winning, it was a significant win for us really, our first with the GTO."

COMTE GIOVANNI VOLPI DI MISURATA
Le Mans

"The first two GTOs were supposed to be Scuderia Serenissima cars and delivered in time for the Targa Florio. When ATS happened in early 1962 and I got involved Ferrari himself called me and said, 'Forget it. You're not getting them'.

"Chiti, Bizzarini and the others didn't leave, Ferrari threw them out. He made a Soviet purge in forty eight hours. He went berserk and threw out one bunch one day and another bunch twenty four hours later. He was a pretty nasty man. By the end of 1961 I think he knew he was going to get beaten in '62. Maybe he threw them out to save face.

"Bizzarini said, 'Since we can't get a GTO, let's try to do better'. So we did. The Breadvan was made very quickly. From the day the mechanics started dismantling the original GT to the day we turned the key was only ten or fifteen days, in May 1962 and we were ready for Le Mans.

"The work was done in the team workshop and I remember seeing ten men working inside the car, their legs and arms sticking out. Bizzarini dropped the engine, making it dry sump and pulled it back in the chassis. It was lighter than a GTO, faster and hugged the road better. It has always been false when it was said that it had a Testa Rossa engine, it never did.

"At Le Mans Chinetti protested and the organisers tried to keep us out of the race but we had a right to be in the GT category because the car was a transformed SWB. The scrutineers told us the car was not properly painted, so we had to repaint it and of course extra paint added weight. Then they made us put a wiper on the back window.

"After the protest we chose to go into the Prototype class but we could have insisted on being in GT. It seemed that the Le Mans organisers were very annoyed at the car. The proving of the car came in the race, if one looks at the lap charts it was way beyond the GTOs and only broke down because in the transformation the propeller shaft had not been balanced and it snapped.

"Otherwise the car was much faster than the GTO and with only four gears. The station wagon shape was very good, when the Ford J car appeared three years later it looked exactly like the Breadvan except that it was rear engined.

"The car was only raced again at Brands Hatch and Montlhery, but it also went to the hillclimb at Ollon Villars. There were two or three GTOs entered but after we arrived they decided not to take part. The car had even more of an advantage on the hillclimb because of its light weight and Abate won. By the

end of the year the Breadvan became less competitive as the GTO was developed. So for 1963 we used only GTOs and I used it as my road car."

MINNEY
Le Mans

"The BRP car was partly prepared at the workshops at F. English. Ron Chubb and I did the car for them but we didn't go to Le Mans with it. During the race the valve clearances closed up on the car and I suppose if the team had known the engine well enough they could have done something about it.

"In a way I don't think the GTO was a really important car for BRP, they were into Grand Prix racing and sports racing cars as well so I think perhaps they weren't quite as serious about the GTO. Certainly not as serious about it as we were at Maranello Concessionaires."

IRELAND
Le Mans

"I raced 3305 at Le Mans with Masten Gregory as my co-driver who was also my team mate in the UDT Laystall Grand Prix team that year. We had some trouble with it to begin with but got it quite well up and then had some electrical troubles and finally the starter motor went. Either the mechanics couldn't change it or we didn't have a spare so we retired the car at about four o'clock in the morning which was a shame. If the GTO ran without any trouble, just putting oil and petrol in and changing brake pads and tyres you stood to do very well in the overall results."

BOB GROSSMAN
Le Mans

"I'd always owned 250GT Ferraris going back to 1958 and drove a California at Le Mans and I had a long wheelbase Scaglietti and several short wheelbase cars, all 250 GTs. So when I got to Le Mans somebody said to me, 'I see you've bought a GTO'. I said, 'What's a GTO?, I've never heard of it'. I bought it as a 250GT Berlinetta!

"We were running third overall and we came in to have a universal joint repaired. Alberto and Alfredo

Le Mans 1962: Abate/Davis in the Breadvan. Scuderia Serenissima's outlandish coupe ran into protests and scrutineering difficulties before finally being allowed to race as a 'GT Prototype'.

65

were our mechanics and they had to replace it. They had to cut the transmission tunnel away to get at it. So while one was pouring water on to cool the hot metal the other was repairing it.

"We were in the pits for about three or four laps but we were four laps ahead of the fourth place car. We got back into the race still third overall but on the same lap. After I restarted, as a result of having a hole cut in the tunnel oil was spraying all over the inside of the car.

"Later in the race on the Sunday afternoon, the car wouldn't restart. At Le Mans you can't replace anything so we had to rewind the starter motor coil and that took two hours. I remember thinking, 'Gosh, if only we could have given a little push when nobody was looking'."

JEAN GUICHET
Le Mans

"Towards the end of the race, when I was pressing Hill and Gendebien, Dragoni, the works Ferrari team manager, approached Pierre Noblet and proposed a dead heat finish with the four litre experimental car. We refused and finally took second overall which was without doubt the best result I had in GT racing.

"There were rumours that the offer was made because they were afraid that the lead car was going to run into problems before the finish. But who knows?"

ROY SALVADORI
Peco Trophy Brands Hatch

"The John Coombs GTO had just arrived from the factory. We had very little practice but I think I made a reasonably good time. There were five or six GTOs in the race for good drivers like Parkes, Surtees and Ireland. I liked the car and found it very easy to drive.

"During the race it rained and I've never been terribly keen on wet weather racing. I hadn't driven a twelve cylinder car for years and the GTO surprised me because it was very good in the wet, very progressive on the throttle. I found it very controllable and had great confidence in it.

"I pushed on and passed Innes for third place and seemed to be catching Surtees. Then Surtees spun,

Jean Guichet

Roy Salvadori

Goodwood Tourist Trophy 1962: Innes Ireland's GTO in the pits. The car shows obvious evidence of Ireland's off course excursion during practice. That hair raising incident bent the chassis frame.

he restarted again but it was sufficient for me to get by. I finished second behind Michael. I thought the car was fabulous, it made driving in the wet almost pleasant.

"It was much easier to drive than any other GT car I'd ever been in before and I hoped to have further drives but it turned out to be my only race in the GTO. John Coombs also had a lightweight E type and at the next race, the TT Graham Hill preferred the GTO. I drove the E type, which was also a splendid car but once you'd tried the GTO you were rather spoilt for any other car."

IRELAND
Tourist Trophy, Goodwood

"In practice for the Tourist Trophy I had a brake disc break up going into Lavant. I seem to recall there having been some rain and when I put the brakes on nothing happened, I couldn't stop the car. I was motoring on pretty rapidly but I noticed that there was quite a formidable looking bush slightly to the left so I put the GTO straight at it.

"I knew it wouldn't stop it but I thought it would at least slow me up a bit but I just went up and over

GTO 20th Anniversary meeting and when I told him about the shunt, he laughed and said he'd have to check and see if the chassis is still bent.

"In the race I remember I had to make a late pit stop. One of the peculiarities of the GTO was the fuel gauge, which had a needle which would wave about all the time and a red warning light which would come on when the tank was low but one was never sure exactly how much fuel was still left. I had quite an advantage over whoever was second so I went into the pits for a quick five gallon churn of fuel. It was noticed that the back tyres were just about worn out so while the fuel was going in the mechanics put a fresh pair of wheels on the back. When I got back onto the circuit the handling was bloody awful.

"For the first couple of laps I thought it was because the new tyres needed scrubbing in but far from getting better it got worse. In fact the back wheels were later found to be loose. I'm sure that the mechanics had tightened the spinners up but I suppose it could have been caused by putting cold wheels onto hot hubs. So that's how Graham Hill got so close. I was going as quick as I could without flying off the road.

"Afterwards there was talk about a time penalty because I had missed out the chicane early in the race but it was force majeure, I didn't do it deliberately. It was either that or drive straight through the wall. Nobody protested as far as I know. I wasn't hauled up into the clerk of the course's office and asked what the hell I thought I was doing. It was obvious what I was doing. I was avoiding having a huge great accident.

"I drove that race wearing just an ordinary pair of slacks, a short-sleeved shirt and a pair of slip-on shoes, which I don't think you would be allowed to do today."

MINNEY
Tourist Trophy, Goodwood

"Sometimes in the UK the preparation of the car would be overseen by Nino Florini, who worked for Ferrari looking after the Assistanza, if he was over here but on other occasions we would do it ourselves.

"At the 1962 TT Bowmaker entered a car for John Surtees, who was a works driver. This car and the Maranello GTO were prepared down at the F. English workshops. The Bowmaker car was overseen by

it. Straight ahead of me was a great earth bank going down a slope. I managed to put the car sideways and hold it there. I was going to hit the bank one way or another and I thought it would be a hell of a lot better to hit it going sideways, which I did.

"I didn't hit it all that hard but the impact flattened the side and in fact knocked the chassis out of line. The mechanics did some temporary beating out of the panels but they couldn't do anything about the chassis. So I drove that race with a frame a quarter or half an inch out front to rear. A fellow called Harrison has got the car now. I saw the car at the

Reg Parnell and his team of mechanics and the Maranello car was overseen by Florini. There wasn't a great deal of difference in racing mileage between the two cars or the way in which they had been driven.

"Dear old Nino changed just about everything he possibly could on the engine of our car, a real belt and braces job. The Bowmaker car had very little changed, none of the bearing shells or rings were changed because frankly they didn't need it. The Maranello car was the same but nevertheless Nino wanted it done.

"The upshot of all this was that the Maranello car driven by Parkes was so outpaced by the Bowmaker car during the first two practices that it was a joke really. It wasn't until Michael was maybe halfway through the race before the engine would even pull the sort of revs that John Surtees could get out of his GTO that had had virtually no work done on it.

"So in a way our car was over prepared, the parts changed on the recommendation of Florini from the Ferrari factory whereas on the Bowmaker car the parts were changed on the basis of what their mechanics under Reg Parnell thought they should do. Frankly they were right because their car didn't give any trouble, it performed absolutely beautifully and was capable of pulling much higher revs on the same gear rations.

"After the accident the mechanical repairs on John's car were done at Poole Road and the bodywork was done by Viking Motors out at Christchurch, who used to do all our aluminium bodywork in those days. It was a privately owned business and they had a very good panel beater there who could work in aluminium and, most importantly, he could weld it without mis-shaping it. He used to carry out nearly all of our aluminium body repairs, particularly on the racing and sports cars."

DAVID PIPER
Tourist Trophy, Goodwood

"For a race like the TT with a Le Mans start the GTO was a particularly good car. The doors were large enough to make it easy to get into, the controls came easily to hand and it had a good strong clutch.

"The usual procedure would be to leave the car parked in first gear before the start so that you would not have to hunt around when you had run across

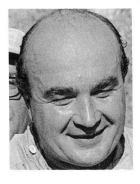

David Piper

Goodwood Tourist Trophy 1962: John Surtees leaves the pits in the Bowmaker Racing GTO. This car, race managed by Reg Parnell, was leading when Surtees collided with Jim Clark's Aston Martin.

Tour de France 1962: Piper/Margulles in Piper's own GTO, chassis 3767GT. They finished fifth overall, at one stage Piper cooled while driving by bottles of water being poured over his head.

the road. Then all you had to do was jump in, push the clutch, turn the key, press the starter, give it four and half thousand revs and slide away into the race."

JACQUES SWATERS
Tour de France

"We had two cars in Rouen for Bianchi/Dubois and Berger/Darville. About two hours before the start Berger was fixing something in the boot of his car with an elasticated strap when it slipped and the metal hook hit him in his eye. So I called Langlois who was in Brussels and he arrived just in time and did the Tour de France at a moment's notice.

"Going from the Nurburgring to Spa, Langlois broke the front suspension. He got to the parc ferme at Spa but under the rules we were not allowed to repair the car. There was half an hour for everyone to practice and set a time for the grid but you had to complete at least three laps. On the old Spa circuit going down to Malmedy there was a little road leading off the track so I sent my mechanics there with a complete front suspension; wishbones, shock absorbers, everything. I said to Langlois: 'When practice starts get to the road and there will be three mechanics waiting there for you, then get back to the pits as soon as possible.'

"It took them twenty minutes to change the suspension, which normally takes one or two days in the garage, but of course we had not completed three laps to qualify. However, I had written down: Car no. 150-3'2".7, 3" 26".2, and so on. When practice finished and the grid sheet was issued I couldn't see my car. So I went furiously to the timekeepers and said, 'What have you done, you've missed my car three times. Look these are the times.'

"There was a lot of confusion and discussion but everyone agreed that I was such a good timekeeper that they must have made a mistake and so they admitted that they must have missed the car!

"Later in the Tour I went back in a hurry to Brussels during the night to get a windshield because Lucien Bianchi had broken his in the accident when he crashed into a milk lorry. I had telephoned to say I was coming and when I arrived they had taken the windshield out of another car we had in the garage so I loaded up, turned around and drove straight back.

"I reached Rheims, where we were trying to repair the car overnight, just a few hours before the race. We fixed it more or less but it was disqualified because the repaired body did not conform to the regulations. We were leading at the time by a long distance."

GUICHET
Tour de France

"At the end of the Hunaudieres straight at Le Mans I was one of three GTOs going line abreast into Mulsanne corner. Lucien Bianchi on my right was obstructed by a slow Alfa Romeo and moved over hitting my front wing and throwing me into Henri Oreiller on my left who spun into the sand ditch on the outside of the corner.

"The damaged front wing was rubbing on my front tyre but I didn't want to stop at the pits to straighten it as I would lose too much time. By the time I finished the race the tyre was badly worn and ready to burst at any moment.

"Later, on the Col d'Aspin hillclimb I took off too fast and brushed against a rock at the side of the road, bending the rim of my left front wheel and breaking the steering rack on the same side. I continued the climb leaving tyre tracks all over the place. At the finish we changed the damage wheel but it wasn't until we put it in the trunk that it finally burst.

"Wanting to make up some time to allow us to repair the front axle I took off rapidly on the narrow road going over the Col de Tourmalet. Coming down the other side at high speed I found myself facing a truck. I stood on the brakes but the disconnected left front wheel steered me straight into the truck. My Tour ended right there."

MINNEY
Autosport Three Hours Snetterton

"This was the first race at which we needed to fit nightlights and illuminated numbers on the car. Ronnie Hoare chose some navigation lights from a boat which I thought was pretty neat."

1962

DONALD McLEOD
Autosport Three Hours, Snetterton

"The car had been back to the factory for a rebuild and we tried to get it on an aeroplane back to England but couldn't. So Michael Parkes said, 'I'll drive it back'. I said, 'You must be made, nine hundred miles across Europe in a car with a straight exhaust'.

"Nevertheless, he drove all the way from the Ferrari factory in Maranello to Snetterton for the race arriving about one o'clock in the morning. By the time Michael got to Snetterton he was stone deaf from the noise of the exhaust so we had to write notes on paper to communicate with him for that meeting. Needless to say he won the race."

MINNEY
Paris 1000 kilometres

"It was our first trip abroad as a team and it was a bit of a culture shock for some of us. It wasn't too bad for me but even I thought the hotel was a bit borderline. When you bear in mind that we had very little sleep leading up to going off.

"We'd not only got the customer cars to look after in the workshop during the working week, we'd also got to go racing at weekends and to come back after the racing and get the customer cars sorted out as well. We were pretty tired quite honestly so a nice bed in a nice hotel room was really quite important to us, even though we weren't there for very long. The hotel that we were booked into was awful, absolutely awful.

"We had weak synchromesh on second gear and we had to strip the gearbox down underneath the banking in one of those boxes they called the pits. I did the gearbox because through misfortune on Ron Chubb's part we actually had had to take a 250GT gearbox to bits in the workshop at F. English and I had helped him do it. Because of that I got the job of sorting it out and putting a new synchromesh in it.

"It was quite a tricky and complicated operation to get the rails out of the top of the box that operated the gears on the mechanism. I was puzzling it out because I'd only done it once before when Florini came along.

"At this stage they had never actually had a GTO gearbox in parts at the Assistanze so it was completely new ground for him. I remember dear old Nino trying to juggle these selector forks in a particular way in order to be able to release them and push them back. After a while he gave up and went away, when he came back I had taken it all to bits.

"I spoke very little Italian or French so the only way we could converse was by drawing on a piece of paper and by hand descriptions. I was so tired, pretty hungry and fed up with the hotel and everything else. When I'd got about a third of the way through trying to explain the sequence and where to push the selector fork in order to be able to get it out I just gave up, I'd had enough.

"In the race I think the misfire was caused by the HT leads breaking down."

VOLPI
Paris 1000 kilometres

"We managed to buy a GTO later in the year. There were lots on order from the factory so you could call the buyer and ask if he wanted to sell it. Some people wanted to get rid of them even before taking delivery.

"This car we took to the Paris race and the revelation there was Bordeu, who was Fangio's pupil. He was teamed up with Berney. In practice Bordeu did just one flying lap and was third fastest overall behind Rodriguez and Mairesse.

"Montlhery was a complicated circuit and he had never driven there before, only an exceptional driver can do that. He never got to drive the car in the race because Berney, who was not a very good driver, did the first shift and broke the car.

"Bordeu used to drive circles around Jim Clark in Formula Junior when Clark was with Lotus and he was with Stanguellini. He was really a new Fangio and destined for Formula One. Colin Chapman took him on later and he had a big accident testing an Elite which put him in hospital for a year. Then he had another racing accident in Argentina which put him out for another year. Two accidents like that really destroys a driver's morale and he gave up. But at the time I think he was better than anyone around."

CHARLIE HAYES
Bridgehampton

"In 1962 I was still racing an SWB Berlinetta and Luigi Chinetti called me and asked me if I was intending to go to Bridgehampton. I said that I didn't see any sense in taking a car like that up there. He said, 'Well I'd like you to come and drive for me in a GTO'.

"For a young racing driver who was trying to get ahead that was a dream come true. So I said, 'Who do I have to kill? ... I'd be happy to go'.

"So I went up there, got to the event for the first practice day and it was a gorgeous GTO, a beautiful motor car. I got myself fitted into the seat and talked to the mechanics who I knew from other tracks I'd been to. After a while Ed Hugus wandered up and said, 'Hi Charlie, what are you doing here?' I said, 'Well, Luigi asked me to come and drive.'

"He said, 'Really, what car?'

'This one'.

'No, I'm driving this'.

'No, no, I'm driving this one'.

'No, no, I'm driving this one'.

"Chinetti had decided, unbeknown to Ed that he wanted what he thought might be a quicker driver in the car for the event. As it turned out I was quicker by a considerable amount because Ed was really a long distance driver and my forte was sprint racing. We had two different styles.

"Typical of Chinetti at that time was the fact that the car actually belonged to a privateer owner and raced under the auspices of the North American Racing Team. The owner was a friend of Ed Hugus so the plot thickened. He arrived later and he said, 'I know Charlie Hayes and how fast he can go, I'd just as soon have him in the car. But I don't want to screw Ed out of the ride.'

"So we both ended up driving the car. In a three hundred kilometre race it was just not a long enough race to do a driver change but they decided that we would do that anyhow. It was decided that I would start the race.

"I was able to stay with Grossman, who was very good especially at Bridgehampton but I managed to get by him just before we pitted. He said later that he had let me by because we were both about to stop and that Hugus would be taking over from me

so it didn't really matter.

"I led for a couple of laps and came in to hand over. Poor Ed was about ten seconds a lap slower and after about eight laps Chinetti spoke to the owner of the car and said, 'Let's put Hayes back in'.

"So I got back in and finished the race. It was a fairly typical Chinetti story, lots of confusion. Every event I ever did with NART seemed to have all sorts of political intrigue.

"My fondest impression of that era was that the GTO was a car that made you look very good. I could really shine because the car was so damn good. One of the sweetest racing cars I ever drove. Very easy to go quick in and confidence inspiring. And of course it made all the right noises."

GROSSMAN
Bridgehampton

"The day before they had a World Championship race for small displacement GTs, 1300cc and under. Cunningham had a team of Abarths which were favourites to win. I thought it would be great to give them a run for their money. A friend of mine had an Abarth which he used on the road so I asked if I could borrow it.

"My mechanic Jim McGee worked on it and I entered the race and won it overall. I beat the Cunningham team. So I went out to celebrate. It was a hell of a victory, Hansgen who I'd beaten was my idol as far as drivers were concerned. I had quite a few drinks and the next day I was hung over and thought, 'Jesus, I've got to drive another race!'

"It was quite a long race and I noticed that a lot of cars had two drivers so I thought I'd better look for a co-driver. I couldn't find anyone suitable so I drove by myself with a hangover and won again. I was beaten only by Rodriguez who was in the sports category but I won the GT class."

PIPER
Rand Nine Hours

"I shipped the car over from Southampton to Cape Town and then drove it on the desert road from Cape Town to Kyalami which is a distance of around a thousand miles.

"In the race I drove with Bruce Johnstone whom I

had met when I raced a Lotus in Formula One. There was rain and our spare wheels had been lost in transit so Lupini, a Ferrari enthusiast based in Johannesburg took the wheels from his own Ferrari road car in the paddock to allow us to finish the race.

"After the Rand Nine Hours I put the car on a boat at Cape Town and sent it to Luanda for the Angola Grand Prix. This was a very colourful race with a great atmosphere. The Portuguese organisers were very enthusiastic and paid the expenses of the overseas competitors."

SWATERS
Angola Grand Prix

"Lucien won the race in 3527. It was good fun to go to Angola, the starting money was very good and travel expenses were paid. That was the period when Sabena had a sticker saying. 'By Sabena you would be there already.'

"They transported the cars and team for free because they were making a promotion on African airlines. It was always good to be leaving Brussels in the winter when it was cold in December and we would spend a few days there going on safari, swimming in the warm ocean and eating lobster. It was, of course, before independence and the Portuguese were very friendly.

"Practice was at five o'clock in the morning on the Friday with the race on Sunday. One of our cars was very badly damaged on the way from the garage where we were based to the track. The chief mechanic was driving when a tool case or something fell onto the accelerator and the car went WHUMP around a palm tree! When we were there we had few spare parts but we rebuilt the car in one day and one night with local help."

JOHN MECOM
Nassau Tourist Trophy

"I bought a Ferrari GTO for Roger Penske to drive at Nassau in the Bahama Tourist Trophy Race and the Ferrari factory gave us the wrong car. They gave us a factory car that had been prepared for racing at the factory in Italy.

"It's usually impossible to get hold of a good racing car from Ferrari if they know it's gonna be used to race against them. Their factory cars are always tuned a little better than their customers' cars. But we were

lucky and got one.

"The night before the race they realised what had happened and they tried to get the car back. We stayed up until two o'clock in the morning arguing with them, and finally they said that my cheque hadn't cleared at the bank so the car wasn't mine. But I knew the cheque had cleared; so we kept the car. Roger did three warm up laps in it, won the race and set a record."

HAYES
Nassau Tourist Trophy

"Bandini drove the car on Sunday in the Nassau Trophy and I drove it on the Friday in the Tourist Trophy for GT cars only. It was wet but the GTO was a marvellous car in the rain. It was a real tropical storm but the car just stuck like glue.

"Bandini and I got to know each other quite well. We spent a lot of time chatting at parties. I took him to the Playboy club in Miami, he was just killer handsome and the Playboy bunnies just fell all over the guy. That was a lot of fun, of course Bandini was in seventh heaven with all these gorgeous girls around him.

"That meeting was very encouraging for me and my career because he was a Grand Prix driver and at that stage I was aspiring to be a good racing driver but I hadn't had all that much experience, it was only the third or fourth year I'd driven but I was able to go as quickly as Lorenzo and in some cases a little faster. That really pleased me."

1963

1

INTRODUCTION

The double championship format was continued in 1963 with an expanded GT series again running alongside the four race GT prototype series which had been renamed as the FIA Challenge Mondial de Vitesse et Endurance.

The GT series was to include hillclimbs and rallies in addition to circuit and road races. The Tour de France and Weisbaden Rally, both rounds of the European Rally Championship would henceforth also carry points towards the GT Manufacturers' crown, as would the Consuma, Freiburg-Schauinsland and Ollon-Villars rounds of the European Mountain Championship.

The GT Championship Divisions were now to be subdivided into three classes, Division III split into 2001 - 2500cc., 2501 - 3000cc. and over 3000cc. As in 1962 points would be awarded to the first six finishers in the Division, irrespective of class.

To be eligible to score points in the GT Championship, a manufacturer would have to compete in six of the 11 races, one of the two rallies and two of the three hillclimbs.

A co-efficient based on various criteria would load the points from the various events. A co-efficient of one would be applied to races of 500 - 750kms. or three to five hours duration, a co-efficient of two to races of 751 - 1500kms. or five to ten hours duration, a co-efficient of three to longer races. Hillclimbs were all deemed co-efficient one events as were rallies containing less than 500kms. of special stages. Rallies having 501 - 1000kms. of special stages would have a co-efficient of two, longer rallies a co-efficient of three.

In other words, of the 16 events on offer, Sebring, Le Mans and the Tour de France would be worth 27 points to the highest placed Division III manufacturer while four other events would carry double points.

1963 GT Championship - Division III	
17.02.63	Intercontinental 3 Hours, Daytona USA (1)
23.03.63	12 Hours of Sebring USA (3)
05.05.63	Targa Florio, Piccolo Madonie, Sicily I (2)
12.05.63	Spa Grand Prix, Francorchamps B (1)
19.05.63	ADAC 1000Kms. Nurburgring D (2)
02.06.63	Consuma hillclimb I (1)
15.06.63	
16.06.63	24 Heures du Mans, Le Mans F (3)
04.07.63	
07.07.63	Weisbaden Rally D (2)
07.07.63	Auvergne Trophy, La Charade F (1)
11.08.63	Freiburg - Schauinsland hillclimb D (1)
24.08.63	Tourist Trophy, Goodwood GB (1)
25.08.63	Ollon Villars hillclimb CH (1)
08.09.63	Coppa Inter Europa, Monza I (1)
15.09.63	Double 500, Bridgehampton USA (1)
14.09.63	
22.09.63	Tour de France F (3)
20.10.63	Paris 1000Kms., Montlhery F (2)

In the event the Paris 1000Kms. was cancelled so there were only three double points events, one of which was a rally. The GT Prototype Championship continued as the same four races as in '62.

To successfully defend its GT crown Ferrari clearly required little alteration to the basic GTO recipe. However, Ferrari did produce a new GT Prototype, the 330LMB, based on the experience of the 4.0 litre GTO seen at the 'Ring and Le Mans in '62.

The 330LMB carried the same 4.0 litre engine fitted with six Weber 42DCN carburettors and with the compression ratio raised to 9.0:1, the result a solid 400b.h.p. at 7,500r.p.m. The Prototype's multi tubular steel frame chassis followed GTO practice but with the wheelbase extended to 2500mm. The transmission was via the same non-synchromesh four speed gearbox found in the 4.0 litre GTO.

The 330LMB's bodywork was a combination of rounded 'Anteater' GTO nose and 250GT Lusso bonnet, cabin and tail. Above the rear arches were raised rectangular pods open at either end to allow added tyre clearance and cooling. A surprising feature of this car was lack of a rear spoiler.

Le Mans Test Weekend 1963: the prototype 330LMB, chassis 4381. Driven by Mairesse, this car was no less than four seconds inside the lap record set the previous year by a sports-racing Ferrari.

1963 GTO RIVALS

As we have seen, Salvadori and Cunningham finished fourth at Le Mans in '62 in a works prepared E Type entered by Cunningham, ahead of the E Type of Lumsden and Sargent. The potential of Jaguar's GT car was obvious. Using knowledge gained from its 1960 Le Mans car and an E Type run in British races in '61 and '62 by John Coombs, the factory produced a small production run of a racing version. This had a aluminium body, various other lightweight parts, a ZF five speed gearbox and an alloy block, Lucas fuel injected engine increasing power to around 300b.h.p.

The factory produced E Type was one major British challenger for the GTO in 1963. Another to throw down the gauntlet was Aston Martin. After its triumphant 1959 season in which it won the World Sportscar Championship, Aston Martin withdrew and concentrated on racing its Grand Prix car in the Formula One World Championship. 1960 turned out to be a disaster for the team as its move into Grand Prix racing, made in 1959, had coincided with the Cooper instigated revolution which effectively killed off the front-engined Formula One car. Aston Martin didn't build a rear-engined replacement: before the end of its second Formula One season it withdrew from competition altogether.

The Aston Martin DB4 introduced in 1958 to replace the DB3 and its successful variants eventually became one of the fastest four-seater production cars in the world. Five different versions of the car were produced, the DB4GT and its Zagato-bodied counterpart finding most favour in racing circles.

All versions of the car were based on a pressed steel platform on to which was welded a tubular steel framework, light alloy body panels attached to the frame forming a rigid outer skin. The chassis was equipped with wishbone and coil spring front suspension and a live rear axle located by trailing arms and a Watts linkage.

The DB4GT was powered by a 3670cc. straight six engine with twin overhead camshafts mated to a four-speed David Brown transmission and was capable of over 140m.p.h., the Tadek Marek-designed motor producing 302b.h.p. at 6000r.p.m.

A low-key racing programme for the car in 1959 saw it win at Silverstone in the hands of Stirling Moss and make an early retirement from Le Mans. Subsequent racing forays were made by private teams, most notably John Ogier's Essex Racing Team, which ran DB4GTs with Zagato bodies for Jim Clark, Roy Salvadori and Innes Ireland. However, the DB4GT was rarely a match for the Ferraris that dominated GT racing.

At the end of 1961 a decision was taken by the factory to return to racing, mainly at the instigation of Aston Martin dealers around the world. In 1962 Le Mans regulations allowed prototypes with engines up to 4.0 litres and plans were made to produce a car for this class.

The resulting car type numbered DP212 was based on the standard platform chassis with the wheelbase marginally increased. The front suspension was essentially unchanged from the DB4 but the rear end was fitted with a De Dion tube hung on torsion bars. Girling disc brakes were mounted on each hub. The engine capacity was increased to 3996cc. by increasing the bore from 92 to 96mm., the stroke remaining at 92mm.

Running on three Weber 50 DCO twin choke carburettors, a power output of 327b.h.p. at 6000r.p.m. was claimed with a 9:1 compression ratio. The transmission was a highly-developed version of the five-speed DBR2 gearbox. The body - an aerodynamically refined version of the DB4GT shell - was made from an alloy of magnesium and aluminium to save weight.

Its 4.0 litre engine ensured that Aston Martin would be near to the front of the starting line up at Le Mans:

in 1962 cars were still assembled in order of engine capacity rather than practice times. Graham Hill shared the one-off DP212 with Grand Prix B.R.M. teammate Richie Ginther and the Englishman led away from the start. He was passed by a Ferrari on the second lap. Electrical problems slowed the car later and a piston failure finally forced its withdrawal after six hours. DP212 was subsequently used as the test bed for three cars to be built by the factory for 1963.

Testing both on the track and in a wind tunnel resulted in a new shape for the tail, which included a spoiler on the trailing edge. Two cars type numbered DP214 were to run in the GT category as developments of the DB4GT as allowed by Appendix J of the International Sporting Code, while a one-off DP215 would run in the prototype class.

The GT cars were obliged by the regulations to run with essentially the same suspension and transmission as the standard DB4GT. The chassis was lightened where possible and the improved DP212 body was fitted. The engine was increased in capacity from the standard configuration to 3750cc., along with modifications to the valves and crankshaft.

Running the same carburettor set up as DP212 and with the compression ratio increased to 9.1:1, the GT engine produced 317b.h.p. at 6000 r.p.m. For the Prototype class, DP215 was fitted with the same 4.0 litre engine as the 1962 car, which was then rated 360b.h.p. at 650r.p.m. with a 9.5:1 compression ratio.

A new box section steel frame chassis for DP215, drilled for lightness, featured all-round independent suspension of wishbones and coil springs. The transmission was unusual in that it was a combined gearbox and final drive unit on the rear axle, as previously used by Aston Martin on its DBR1 sports racing car.

Aside from the new GT opposition provided by the Lightweight E Type and the DP214 Aston Martin, in 1963 the GTO would also face an American challenger. Of course, the basis of Carroll Shelby's famed Cobra was a 1953 vintage ladder frame chassis built by A.C. Cars Limited of Thames Ditton.

Lauded as the first British sportscar of the post-war period with all round independent suspension, the AC Ace, introduced in October 1953, was powered by the company's own straight six engine which had a bore of 65mm. and a stroke of 100mm. giving a 1991cc. capacity.

The chassis and body were to a design by John Tojeiro, the frame formed from two large diameter longitudinal tubes with smaller diameter cross tubes. Suspension was via lower wishbones and transverse leaf springs at each corner with 11" Girling hydraulic drum brakes front and rear. The body was based on a contemporary Ferrari design.

Tojeiro had sold a number of these chassis to private owners to race with a variety of engines before AC bought the design and marketed it as the Ace. In 1955 the venerable AC motor was replaced by the more powerful 1971cc. pushrod Bristol straight six engine with triple Solex carburettors, reckoned to produce 128b.h.p. at 5500r.p.m. 11.5" disc brakes were fitted at the front and the Ace was campaigned thus for the next five seasons taking a 2.0 litre class win at Le Mans in 1957 in the hands of Rudd and Bolton.

In 1960 a 2553cc. in line six cylinder Ford Zephyr engine was fitted to the chassis owned by Ken Rudd. Running on three SU carburettors, the 170b.h.p. it produced at 5500r.p.m. was delivered to the road through a Moss four speed gearbox. Following a number of successes, the factory introduced a production version of this car.

Around this time Carroll Shelby, recently retired from racing, was looking for a chassis with which to enter the sports car market in the United States. Having considered various options Shelby struck a deal with AC. Over the winter of 1961-62 an Ace chassis was fitted with the 4262cc. (221cu.in.) Ford Fairlane V8 engine with single Holley carburettor, producing 260b.h.p. at 6500r.p.m. The engine was mated to a four speed Borg Warner transmission feeding through a Salisbury differential.

After testing in America, and following strengthening of the chassis by the use of thicker tubes and the introduction of hub mounted 12" disc brakes all round, the AC Cobra went into production. The first seventy-five off the production line were fitted with the 4.2 litre Fairlane engine while later examples were manufactured with a 4727cc (289cu.in.) version giving 300b.h.p. at 5750r.p.m.

The Cobra made its competition debut at Riverside in California in October 1962 but the car retired with a hub failure. Over the following winter the teething troubles were rectified. The Cobra bared its fangs at Daytona in 1963 and gave the Prancing Horse a fright...

GTO RACE RECORD

The GT series opened in Florida in February. On the day before the championship race at Daytona a 250-mile race was held in which Fireball Roberts' was the best-placed GTO in fourth place overall. David Piper in 3767 on another intercontinental adventure also raced, while Ireland practised in 3589 but did not start.

The following day's championship counter, the Daytona Three hours, was won by Pedro Rodriguez who was returning after a temporary retirement following his brother's death in practice for the Mexican Grand Prix in November 1962. Rodriguez drove to victory in a new car, 4219, entered by NART and owned by 19-year-old Mamie Reynolds, and he won despite a 50-second penalty for remaining in the car during a refuelling stop. Roger Penske was second in Mecom's car.

Piper's green car spun off on oil and was eventually classified 21st at the finish; Ireland in the Rosebud car went out with a punctured tyre, while Roberts could only manage 15th place. The race was of great significance in that it marked the international competition debut of Carroll Shelby's Ford V8-powered Cobra. Driven by Dave McDonald, the rumbling monster was disputing second place with Penske until a water hose split. After repairs the Cobra finished fourth behind Dick Thompson in a Chevrolet Corvette.

The opening round of the Speed and Endurance challenge, the Sebring 12 hours, received entries for six GTOs and a 330LMB. Sharing with brewery heir Augie Pabst, Penske took fourth place overall and won the GT category, having held second in the early laps. The Mecom car finished behind three Ferrari Experimentals as the challenge from the Cobras, lightweight E Types and local Corvettes fell apart.

Abate/Bordeu in 3445, now owned by Centro Sud, was entered by the Republic of Argentina, Bordeu

being protege of Fangio. They finished fifth overall. Ginther/Ireland took sixth place for Rosebud after an early stop to replace a water hose. Bonnier/Cannon were 13th in the Daytona winning car, having its last international outing. The car was later drag raced by Mamie Reynolds herself before being sold and run by its new owner in some minor American events in 1964.

Piper/Cantrell were 14th in 3767, which Ed Cantrell bought from its English owner after the race. Hayes/Thieme were 18th at the finish. The 4.0 litre 330LMB, driven by Parkes and Bandini, crashed during the fifth hour and was retired with a split fuel tank.

At the Le Mans test weekend in April, Willy Mairesse set the fastest time in a 330LM, no less than four seconds below the lap record set by a sports racing prototype. The 330LM was also driven by Parkes, who was little slower than the Belgian.

The Goodwood International Trophy meeting GT race was won by Parkes in 3647, which had been borrowed back by Maranello Concessionaires from its new owners, Tommy Hitchcock and Russian Prince Zourab Tchkotoua, after the delivery of the team's new car was delayed. Graham Hill was second in a lightweight E Type, preferring it to John Coombs' GTO 3729 in which he also practised.

Seven GTOs entered the Targa Florio: Maurizio Grana and Gianni Bulgari were fourth overall and GT winners in 3413 which had been used as a works training car on the 1962 Targa, after which it was sold to Eduardo Lualdi, who used it for hillclimbs and minor Italian races and won the three litre class of the 1962 Italian GT Championship. In April 1963 the car was sold to Bulgari and it was entered for the Sicilian race by Scuderia Centro Sud. Grana was actually third on the penultimate lap but eased off when it started to rain, mindful of having thrown

Goodwood Tourist Trophy 1963: Graham Hill lifts a wheel on his way to victory. The reigning World Champion recovered from a spin with Ireland's Aston Martin to head Parkes's sister car home.

away a class lead the year before, and was overtaken by a Porsche sports racing car on the run in to the finish.

Bordeu/Scarlatti were sixth in 4091 owned by Bettoja, Hitchcock and Tchkotoua's ex-Maranello car was eighth, Nicolosi/Taramazzo were 13th in the ex-Guichet Le Mans GT winner 3705, owned by Nicolosi and entered by Scuderia San Marco. Scuderia Filipinetti's 3909, shared by Bourillot/de Bourbon Parme, was crashed and Norinder/Troberg in Norinder's ex-SSR car 3445 failed to finish, while Von Csazy's 3809 was crashed in practice by Andrew Hedges, who was having his first drive in a GTO and making his Targa debut one that he would not forget...

In the GT race at the Silverstone International Trophy meeting, Parkes in Coombs' GTO 3729 battled fiercely with Graham Hill and Salvadori in lightweight E Types until he spun off and hit the earth bank, damaging the Ferrari's nose on the 21st of 25 laps.

The Spa Grand Prix was a new round of the GT Championship and attracted four GTOs and two Drogo-bodied specials. The race on the blindingly fast triangle of public roads was won by Mairesse by over a minute in 3757, which had been sold by Dernier to Ancez but was still entered by Ecurie Francorchamps. The Belgian set a new GT lap record at 127.41 m.p.h. for good measure.

Noblet was second in his own car, 3943, ahead of Swiss driver Joseph Siffert in the Filipinetti car, which had been second fastest in practice to Mairesse. Piper was left at the start in Cantrell's 3767 and failed to finish.

Gerald Langlois van Ophem was fourth in 2053GT, the car tested in September 1961 by Moss, with GTO body modifications. After fitting with a regular 250GT body it had been sold to Ecurie Francorchamps in early 1962 and had crashed at the ADAC 1000kms. It then went to Modena to be rebodied by Piero Drogo, the design combining the nose of the original Breadvan with the tail of the Kerrison car. It was raced at the Angola Grand Prix late in 1962 but was damaged on the return sea journey and went back to Modena for repair.

Kerrison was fifth in 2735, the ex-Rob Walker car driven to victory in the 1961 Tourist Trophy by Moss before being sold to Kerrison in 1962 and crashed at the TT by Robin Benson. This car also went to

Targa Florio 1963: Scarlatti/Bordeu drove Scuderia Serenissima's GTO, chassis 3445GT. The pair finished sixth overall, second in Division III GT. This car was later sold to Swedish driver Ulf Norinder.

Modena for a Drogo body, made in this instance by Neri and Bonaccini.

Heavy rain was a major feature of the ADAC 1000kms. at the Nurburgring. The race was won by Surtees and Mairesse in an open-top works 246SP Experimental, nearly nine minutes ahead of Noblet/Guichet in Noblet's 3943. "Elde" (Leon Dernier)/Langlois van Ophem were fifth in the Francorchamps Drogo Special, Piper/Cantrell were sixth in 3767 and Kerrison/Salmon were eighth in 2735.

Walter/Muller retired Filipinetti's 3909 with valve problems at quarter distance. Von Czasy, sharing 3809 with Karl Foitek, crashed his GTO in practice and the race, rolling it into retirement. American Tommy Hitchcock suffered a similar fate, putting his car (shared with Tchkotoua) onto its roof in the Karrusel banking, closing it off for the remainder of the race. The Nurburgring event saw another challenge to Ferrari's continuing domination of the big capacity GT class. Noblet/Guichet had to stave off a threatening E Type - until the Jaguar blew its engine.

In an inauspicious start to the inclusion of hillclimbs in the GT Championship, an event held over the Passo del Consuma, 20 kilometres east of Florence, was poorly supported by GT manufacturers' representatives. Ferrari took maximum points in Division III thanks to the efforts of Paulo Colombo in 3851GT, this being the car crashed by Oreiller at Montlhery in the autumn of '62. Nicolosi in 3705GT was second in class.

The Goodwood Whitsun Trophy meeting on 3rd June featured a twenty-one lap GT event. Coombs' white car, 3729, was entered for Mike MacDowel who led the first lap until he was passed by Parkes in Maranello Concessionaires' new car, 4399. Kerrison was third in the Drogo special.

At Le Mans it was Aston Martin's turn to hound Ferrari. However, the fastest Aston, in the hands of Ireland/Bruce McLaren, blew up before the six-hour mark and a sister car, which had proved capable of splitting the GTO ranks, failed to last until half-distance.

There were four GTOs and three 330LMBs at Le Mans in 1963, and at half-distance three GTOs were still running, lying third, fourth and fifth behind two Ferrari Experimental sports racing cars and without a class challenger in sight. Tavano/Abate in Scuderia Serenissima's new car 4757 had led the big GT class during the first quarter of the race, until it was crashed during the eighth hour.

At the twelve-hour mark running third was a brand-new, special-bodied NART car (4713) driven by Piper and Masten Gregory. Two hours later this sleek, Pininfarina-styled car with a 330LM-type body, fell behind the gamely pursuing Equipe Nationale Belge machines due to burnt-out dynamo bushes. A little later, further time was lost when Gregory went off the road at Arnage in his hurry to make up ground and had to dig the car out of a sandbank. Nevertheless, 4713 eventually finished, sixth.

The Belgian Ecurie Francorchamps GTOs, both new cars, had far less trouble and wound up sandwiching the second, sick sports racer. Beurlys and Langlois van Ophem in Dernier's 4923 finished less than 200 kilometres behind the winner, while Pierre Dumay/"Elde" drove Dumay's 4153 into fourth place.

The delighted Belgians celebrated in grand style on the Sunday night and then drove the class winning car to Paris to enjoy the nighlife of the French capital on Monday evening, finally returning the somewhat hard-worked machine home on the Tuesday.

Of the trio of 330LMs, Noblet/Guichet in 4381 went out with oil pump failure in the seventh hour, while Dan Gurney and Jim Hall in the NART car 4453, which had held fifth place after six hours, went out with broken half shaft in the tenth hour. Michael Salmon and Jack Sears brought the only surviving 330LM home in fifth place, having been under the strict orders of Maranello Concessionaires' patron Colonel Ronnie Hoare to bring the works-loaned chassis to the finish.

The 25-lap Sports and GT race supporting the French Grand Prix at Rheims saw three GTOs beaten by Abate in the SSR Testa Rossa and Dick Protheroe's Lightweight E Type. Lucien Bianchi was third in Ecurie Francorchamps' 4293, Noblet fourth in 3943. David Piper's new chassis, 4491, appeared - this car featuring a lowered roofline. In the race it got caught up in confusion surrounding Simon's accident in a 5.0 litre Maserati 151 Experimental.

The Martini International Silverstone organised by the Aston Martin Owners' Club gave Parkes an easy win in 4399 in a race reduced from 52 to 30 laps by rain. Parkes had lapped the entire field by lap 19 and was close to lapping the whole field twice by the time the race was stopped.

The Weisbaden Rally held on the 4th to the 7th of July was nominally a round of the GT Championship but was ignored by the manufacturers since the regulations required participation in only one of the two rallies on the calendar and the Tour de France was the other rally on offer. Incidentally, Division III on the Weisbaden event was won by an Austin Healey 3000.

The GT Championship battle resumed with the Auvergne Trophy at Clermont Ferrand on 7th July, a three-hour race. Abate in the SSR 4757 was second fastest in practice ahead of teammate Bandini's Testa Rossa, but he stalled the engine at the start. He had recovered to third by the end of the first hour and hung on to finish in that position, winning the GT class. Piper was ninth behind 2.0 litre class-winning Porsches in sixth and seventh. The circuit was not ideally suited for a car as powerful as the GTO: 51 corners in 5.1 miles cramped its style.

A similar observation could be made of the Mallory Park circuit at which a GT race formed part of the Grovewood Trophy meeting. It was won by Graham Hill's E Type from Sears in the Maranello car. Sears managed to lead initially, until the superior power band of the Jaguar engine told. Salvadori and Peter Sutcliffe were third and fourth in E Types, Piper was fifth ahead of Salmon in Coombs' 3729, recovering from a dice with Sutcliffe during which the white GTO hit the wall at the hairpin, necessitating a stop to check for damage. Kerrison was seventh, Hitchcock eighth.

The British Grand Prix support races included a race for sports and GT cars. Sears was fifth overall and GT winner in the Maranello car ahead of Piper who had led the GT class in the early laps. MacDowel was tenth in the Coombs car. Kerrison retired his Drogo special with engine trouble.

A 6.95 mile section of mountain road between the villages of Freiburg and Schauinsland was the venue for the second hillclimb in the GT Championship. Carlo Mario Abate in the Scuderia Serenissima 4757GT defeated minimal opposition to provide a further maximum Division III points score for Ferrari.

The Guards Trophy at Brands Hatch saw Graham Hill lead from the start in Maranello Concessionaires' 4399 until brake problems caused his retirement. The reigning World Champion drove a GTO since the

Le Mans Test Weekend 1963: two views of the Ecurie Francorchamps Drogo-bodied 250GT. This car combined the nose of the '62 Breadvan with the less adventurous tail of the Kerrison Drogo car.

Brands' scrutineers rejected the lightweight E Type he had originally intended to run. Sears in Coombs' 3729 was fifth and won the GT class from Ireland's ill-handling Aston Martin. Piper took seventh ahead of Bandini in the 330LM 4725 that had finished fifth at Le Mans, the Italian recovering after a spin to win the over three GT class. Kerrison was eighth and Hitchcock 11th, the latter having been black-flagged twice for a loose window.

The English round of the GT Championship, the Tourist Trophy at Goodwood was a contest between the locally-based GTOs. Leading entrants Maranello Concessionaires and John Coombs had joined forces, Coombs' driver. Graham Hill had chosen the '63 Maranello car (4399), leaving Parkes the older Coombs' car (3729). Hill led from the start with Ireland close behind in the works' Aston Martin followed by Parkes. On lap ten Ireland lunged at a gap, causing himself and Hill to spin at Woodcote. Both continued after Parkes had gone through.

Ireland pitted to change flat spotted tyres and re-joined just ahead of Parkes on the road. As the first two cars tried to lap Ireland, Hill slipped past Parkes. Parkes was trapped behind Ireland and after a desperate battle both spun at Woodcote, ending up on opposite sides of the track.

By the time Ireland and Parkes had recovered, Hill led by 12 seconds. Ireland spun again at Woodcote two laps later. Parkes took the lead from Hill at the World Champion's next fuel stop. That stop dropped Hill to fifth. The situation reversed as Parkes made his stop, but he managed to rejoin in second place.

At Hill's second stop, Parkes - only scheduled for one stop - went ahead by 30 seconds. Twenty-five laps later, when Parkes was 10.4 seconds ahead, he slowed to let Hill through to win as prearranged by the team.

Roy Salvadori's E Type Jaguar finished third on the same lap but had never been a threat. The English-based lightweight E Type had inflicted some early season defeats upon the British GTOs in National races but could not reproduce the speed of the German-based Jaguar seen at the 'Ring when it came to the all-important British event.

Piper took fifth with Penske eighth in the NART 4713 330LM-bodied car, after a spin and a some-what leisurely pitstop. On lap sixteen Tommy Hitch-cock had the accident he had looked likely to have

all through the early laps of the race, his car rolling after making hard contact with an earth bank. In fact, 3647 had landed in the same place at which Surtees had gone off in the same car a year earlier. Kerri-son was relieved by Sutcliffe in the Drogo special after the owner suffered burns to his feet. After treat-ment he was able to take over the car again and fin-ished tenth.

On the same weekend as the Goodwood TT the Ollon-Villars hillclimb took place on a twisting 4.97 mile course. In the early Sixties this German event was the jewel in the hillclimbing crown, regularly attracting Grand Prix names. Division III was again won by Abate in SSR's 4757GT, beating Berney in the Scuderia Filipinetti GTO by 25 seconds.

GT points were next up for grabs at the Coppa Inter Europa Three Hours. Parkes in Maranello's 4399 was fastest in the damp practice by four seconds from Ulf Norinder in 3445 and Salvadori's works Project 214 Aston Martin. The bearded Swede led form the start but was soon passed by Parkes and Salvadori. Norinder made an early pitstop to investigate a mis-fire.

After refuelling stops, Parkes and Salvadori were three seconds apart on the road. A tremendous scrap for the lead ensued which was resolved in the last two laps in favour of the Aston. Piper had initially challenged Salvadori but fell away to finish fourth in 4491, behind Bianchi in the second Aston Mar-tin.

Ferdinando Pagliarini was fifth in 3607, a car co-owned by himself and Italiana Petroli, leading home Egidio Nicolosi in Scuderia San Marco's ex-Guichet 3705, ahead of the recovering Norinder. Vincenzo Zanini rolled 3451GT, the '62 Targa GT winner which he had bought from the factory. Salvadori's victory was cheered to the echo by fans who thought he was an Italian!

There was another defeat in store for the GTO before the season was out, this time by a Shelby Cobra. The occasion was the Bridgehampton Double 500 on 14th/15th September 1963, which suffered from poor support by the European teams. In the GT Championship race Grossman/Hayes in a lone GTO finished tenth. In contrast, it was a great day for the Cobra, Dan Gurney and Ken Miles finish-ing first and second to the delight of the locals.

In the following day's non-championship race, Gurney

Le Mans 1963: Dan Gurney in the 330LM he shared with Jim Hall laps the little Rene Bonnet of Beltoise. Entered by NART, sadly the Ferrari retired in the tenth hour when its transmission failed.

finished third in NART's 330LM with Cantrell/Kolb sixth in the ex-Piper 3767. The day of the Bridgehampton race was also the starting day for the Tour de France, upgraded to World Championship status this year. Here most of the quick GTOs were to be found.

Six GTOs and one Drogo special were entered and there were five GTOs in the first five places in the GT category after the Rheims race. Guichet/Behra in Guichet's new car 5111GT led Bianchi/Abate in the SSR 5095, Schlesser/Claude Leguezec in NART's 4713, Bandini/Tavano in SSR's 4757 and the Guido Fossati/Ariberto Francolino 4675GT.

Schlesser over revved his engine to 9400r.p.m. (the limiter was usually set at 8600r.p.m.) and lost time making repairs to a broken valve spring. Trying to make up lost time, he missed two checkpoints and was disqualified. 5095 was badly damaged when crashed by Bianchi in fog and rain during a night road section when a brake pipe came adrift.

Makeshift repairs were effected and, despite having to keep the engine running for fear of not being able to restart, Bianchi actually won three subsequent hillclimb stages. Considering the damage he was lucky not to be disqualified for the second year in succession. By the final race at Monaco the car was in such a state that co-driver Abate was barely able to limp home to claim second place.

Edgar Berney/John Gretener in the Filipinetti 3909 were eliminated with a broken differential, while 4757 crashed and was written off, Tavano suffering a broken arm. 4675 was also crashed and this chassis was rebodied when it was later repaired. Guichet/Jose Behra won the event in the last GTO built before the jigs were dismantled: 5111. Guichet had skilfully saved fuel by slipstreaming rival GTOs during the race stages. Kerrison/Rophard in 2375 retired on the second stage at the Nurburgring with a broken gearbox.

The British season closed in the traditional manner with the Autosport Three Hours at Snetterton. Sears in Coombs' 3729 led from the outside of the front row of the grid but was passed by Clark's Lotus 23 before the end of the first lap. The sports racer won from Parkes in 4399 while Sears slipped to fourth place.

The Canadian Grand Prix on 28th September 1963 for sports racing and GT cars attracted five GTOs. The race was dominated by the type of cars that would eventually contest the Can Am series and a number of well-driven Cobras. Piper finished tenth in 4491 ahead of Mike Gammino in 3387, now owned by Liberto Gerardi; Grossman was 14th in the NART-entered 3223. Grant Clark in Cantrell's 3767 retired with transmission trouble after 14 of 100 laps.

In the Angola Grand Prix, Bianchi was second in

Nurburgring 1000Kms. 1963: the von Csazy/ Foitek GTO, 3809GT, looking rather battered following shunts on the Targa Florio and in practice for this event. Alas, later in the race the car crashed again.

Ecurie Francorchamps' 4153 and Remordu was sixth in the team's sister car, 3757. David Piper took his car out to South Africa again and, sharing with Tony Maggs, won the Rand Nine Hours at Kyalami. 4491 was barged off on to the dirt at the side of the track by a Cobra at the start but Piper took the lead on lap two and was not headed again, other than during early fuel stops. The GTO was 17 laps ahead of the Cobra in second place at the finish.

Mike Gammino was second in the Nassau Tourist Trophy and sixth in the Nassau Trophy to round off the GTO year.

The shock home defeat at Monza and the race forfeited by the recurrent lack of willingness by European teams to travel to Bridgehampton aside, it had been a crushingly successful season for Ferrari in Division III. In terms of points gathering, it was a one horse race in Division III since no other manufacturer undertook the qualification allocation of events. There were, however, ominous warning signs from the Cobra camp that suggested the Americans were deadly determined to wrest the GT crown in '64.

Ferrari was not unduly concerned since it had a new weapon under development that would take care of the Cobra.

Ferrari had produced 37 GTOs from January 1962 to September 1963, including three 4.0 litre cars (the third a road car for Ferrari director Paul Cavalier), the two earlier cars having been sold for the road. No attempt was made to homologate the 330LMB to replace the GTO as Ferrari had announced the 250LM, a pure mid-engined sports racing car with an enclosed cockpit.

Interior trim helped justify its claimed GT status. However, the Italian sporting authority had so far failed to get it accepted as a GT since there was only an intent to build 100 examples over a period of time. Porsche - which had stolen outright victory on the Targa Florio from Ferrari - got its mid-engined 2.0 litre 904 coupe homologated by actually building 100 examples. The GTO had been accepted as an evolution of the 250GT SWB but there could be no such argument for the 250LM and Ferrari did not intend to line up 100 examples straightaway. Instead, it played politics - and into the fangs of the Cobra...

BEHIND

THE WHEEL

IRELAND
Daytona Three Hours

"At the 1963 Daytona Intercontinental the right rear brake disc broke up and of course chewed through the spokes. I went off the road and through a huge advertising hoarding."

HAYES
Sebring 12 hours

"Sebring was a disaster, I started in the car and after about forty minutes, going into a fairly quick righthand corner the brake pedal went to the floor. I went off the road and had to spin the car to keep from running into a stand full of spectators. It scared the hell out of me.

"I went back to the pits and told Luigi that the car was out of brakes and he accused me of using them too much. So I accused him of not having put in fresh pads, as was supposed to have been done before the event. I don't know who was right but it didn't really do my relationship with him much good. I didn't drive another race for him until Sebring in 1964."

SALVADORI
Silverstone International Trophy GT race

"Graham Hill was in the Coombs E type, I was in Tommy Atkin's car and Michael Parkes was in Coombs' GTO, we were all lapping within a fraction of a second of each other the whole time. The GTO was leading and we were pushing Michael. Eventually we pushed him so hard that he lost it at Becketts and then Graham was leading.

"I got a good run at him going through Stowe and passed him on the second to last lap. Graham made a desperate attempt to retake me going into Woodcote and got all screwed up and went onto the grass. So I was happy because I knew all I had to do was get round the last lap.

Silverstone International Trophy meeting 1963: Michael Parkes in Coomb's GTO chassis 3729GT. Parkes uncharacteristically spun off at Becketts towards the end of the race, crumpling the nose.

1963

Targa Florio 1963: Hitchcock/Tchkotowa's ex-Maranello GTO, chassis 3647GT. In their first outing in this car, the American-Russian pairing finished the mountain race a worthy eighth overall.

"By this time I had two seconds on Graham and decided not to take any chances. Going into Becketts I took it even slower than before and lost it myself. By the time I got back on the circuit Graham had gone by.

"We thought we'd pushed Michael into a mistake but there was something peculiar at Becketts, maybe some oil on the road. But that was a race where the E types and the GTO were equal."

GIANNI BULGARI
Targa Florio

"This was my first race with the GTO that I had bought a few weeks earlier from Eduardo Lualdi. My co-driver was Maurizio Grana who had been my co-driver in the other long distance races. Coming to the GTO from the Alfa Romeo Giulietta Zagato we had raced previously, we were a little intimidated by both the car and the competitors among whom were Jean Manuel Bordeu and Giorgio Scarlatti. They had won the GT class in '62 with one of the very first GTOs, the one belonging to Piero Ferraro.

"Giorgio was admiring the watch I was wearing so I said to him, if we finish ahead of you the watch will be yours. By half distance all the official cars from Maranello had retired and we were the leading Ferrari, behind a group of Porsches. From then on we got full support from the factory team pits. At threequarter distance we were leading the GT class when it started to rain. The GTO was quite easy to drive on a dry surface but it was quite a handful in the wet on a twisty road such as the Targa Florio's.

"Linge, with his special Porsche Carrera, overtook us to take third position overall and win the GT class. We finished fourth ahead of the other Ferraris, with Scarlatti and Bordeu in sixth place. So I lost my watch but won the 3.0 litre GT class."

SWATERS
Spa Grand Prix

"Mairesse was driving on the Saturday in England at the International Trophy at Silverstone. He arrived late in the evening after practice. The director of the race, Leo Sven, who was a great friend of mine, arranged a special half hour qualifying session for Willy on Sunday morning. Of course, he made the fastest time by a very long way.

"It was a beautiful sunny day and there was a large

crowd. Sven was afraid of having a race without any interest and that Mairesse would be out on his own for the whole race. So I promised that I would organise something.

"By the middle of the race Mairesse was over half a lap ahead so I stopped him and we changed the wheels. Then the mechanics were working under the car for two or three minutes but there was absolutely nothing wrong at all.

"Willy was standing by the car when the second place man went into the lead so I said 'You must go.' But he said, 'No, we have plenty of time. Let's wait a little longer.'

"When he finally jumped into the car we were far off Noblet in the lead. For the spectators it was fantastic because on each lap he took ten seconds or twelve seconds from the leader. Finally, five laps before the end he passed Noblet and still won the race by over thirty seconds."

MICHAEL SALMON
ADAC 1000 Kilometres

"The Drogo-bodied car was in my opinion a total disaster, a very difficult car for tall people to drive. The actual driving position was appalling, you virtually had to lie down in it and there was no head room at all. Christopher spent a lot of money on it and had the six carburettor conversion done, so engine-wise it went quite well but it didn't have a five-speed gearbox. Furthermore, it didn't handle terribly well, in fact it didn't really handle at all. Not even like a SWB, much less a GTO. It was an absolute pig of a car to drive.

"It was the only time I've almost gone down on my knees and prayed to the Good Lord that we'd never get it running. It broke a halfshaft in practice and I remember being stuck out at the other end of the Nurburgring on a beautiful bright sunny day speaking to the sheep in a field and hoping and praying that this would be the last time I would have to drive the wretched thing...

"Unfortunately, we did get a new half shaft for it and it was repaired in time for the start. It was a miserable race of very mixed weather with a lot of rain showers and sleet. The 'Ring threw practically everything at us that day. The car was very edgy all the time and I spun on the first lap when I took over from Christopher, just past the first series of S

bends after the start.

"The thing spun on me for no apparent reason and I found myself facing the wrong direction behind a blind corner. I thought, 'Well that's it, no way can I do a three-point turn in front of oncoming race cars', so I just sat there. Fortunately a member of the crowd climbed up on top of the fence and gave me directions when there was nothing coming and we did rather well to finish eighth.

"It was the one and only time I ever drove the car. Funnily enough Michael Parkes tested the car for Christopher at Goodwood later on and said that there

Nurburgring 1000Kms. 1963: Salmon/Kerrison drove the latter's Drogo-bodied 250GT. The modified 250GT was difficult to drive and after teething troubles in practice the British pair finished eighth.

was something very far wrong with the handling of it. I don't really know if it was ever put right, I don't think it was."

CHRISTOPHER KERRISON
ADAC 1000 Kilometres

"I remember we took a mechanic to the Nurburgring in 1963 who was rather a strong personality. We'd booked a whole lot of rooms and he and his wife bagged the best one and we didn't dare turf him out. There was a lot of conferring between Michael and I as to whether we should but we finally agreed that

neither of us dared to, so the mechanic got the best room in the hotel.

"That year at the Ring on the last corner leading up to the straight there was a dandelion growing on the apex of the corner at the cutting point. On the day of the race before the start somebody picked the dandelion..."

SWATERS
Le Mans

"We spent four nights without sleeping that year. We had a lot of problems during practice so we worked all night on Friday to fix it. Saturday was spent at the track, of course, and on Sunday there was a big dinner at our hotel after the race and I think we went to bed at five o'clock in the morning. The next day the prize giving was in the afternoon and the A.C.O. had asked me to stay there with the cars because we had won the Trophee du Mans for the best team performance.

"On the Monday evening we set off for Paris, we stopped on the outskirts near Rambouillet to have dinner in a small auberge. When we had finished at about ten o'clock, somebody said, 'Why don't we go to Montmatre?'

"We all thought this was a very good idea so we went with the two GTOs which still had the racing numbers on and dirt from the race and we were in Bois de Nuit in Montmartre until four in the morning. So the cars that had finished second and fourth at Le Mans on Sunday spent the night outside a nightclub on Monday. We got back to Brussels on Tuesday morning as the sun was rising."

Jack Sears

Le Mans 1963: Elde/ Dumay in Ecurie Franorchamps' GTO, chassis 4153GT. In its first race, this car finished a splendid fourth overall. It spent the Monday night after the race outside a nightclub in Paris.

PIPER
Le Mans

"Masten lost an hour digging it out and when he handed over to me the first thing I noticed was that the steering was bent. The wheel was resting in the ten to four position. Driving down the long straight for the first time was like driving in a dust storm, the car was full of sand!"

JACK SEARS
Le Mans

"It was a magical experience driving for the Colonel. Everything had to be perfect and everyone had the best of everything. Being ex-Army, his administrative qualities were of a very high order and this carried through into the racing team. When you drove for the Colonel you wanted for nothing and consequently it was a very happy team.

"The 330LMB was similar to the GTO but had a four-speed crash gearbox which was nothing like as

nice as the GTO box. It also didn't handle as well as the GTO but compared to the Healey I'd driven at Le Mans in 1960, the Ferrari was a step into the next world. The leap forward in performance and handling was huge. The Healey was doing 145 on the straight in 1960 whereas the Ferrari was pulling 175m.p.h. in 1963.

"We were under orders not to stress the cars, the Colonel wanted us to finish. Michael Salmon and I were sufficiently wise to follow the command. We had a chat beforehand and agreed a plan for the race. The plan being to drive sensibly and very smoothly - it paid off.

"We stroked the brakes on at the end of the straight and made comfortable gear changes, double declutching because there was no synchromesh on the crash box and engaging the gear smoothly. Smoothness was of the essence. That race taught me a lot about racing, mainly that the smooth approach gets results."

SALMON
Le Mans

"The 330LMB was a good solid car. It was brought up on the road from the factory by Ronnie Hoare. The first time we ever saw it was when it arrived for practice. Ronnie was a terrific stickler for preparation, his ability and conscientiousness in preparing a car was unrivalled. He was a quite extraordinary person and used to say, 'I'm not interested where the car finishes as long as the drivers are safe and sound.' He always had that in the back of his mind in whatever race he ran cars in.

"The 330LMB had rather poor brakes - like a lot of the Ferraris in those days - and a four-speed gearbox. We had a water pump leak fairly early on which we could do nothing about and therefore when the fuel load was getting lighter on each stint, we had to keep an eye on the water temperature gauge as we were losing water and couldn't drive it as quickly as we could have done if all had been well.

"About 12 o'clock on the Sunday the car was brought in and Ronnie said, 'Change the wheels' but the mechanics couldn't get the left hand rear wheel off because it had turned on its splines. I said, 'This is absurd, we can't possibly withdraw the car because there's still enough tread to go right the way through.

"But Ronnie was insistent, if they couldn't take the wheel off the car would be withdrawn. He was the boss and that was that. Fortunately, we did get the wheel off and we carried on. There was a bit of excitement an hour and a half before the finish. My wife was doing the timing for Ronnie and he was convinced that the Masten Gregory 250GTO was about half a lap behind and catching us. Jean said, 'This is absolute nonsense. They're a lap and a half behind. Don't worry.'

"But when I was put into the car for the last stint Ronnie said, 'As fast as you like Michael, get cracking, just go motor racing.' It was wonderful. I had a terrific last session, flat out with the headlights blazing, storming round the track with Ronnie convinced we were only just ahead of the Gregory car, which in fact was not the case.

"At the end of the race it was very emotional. I switched it off at the finishing line and it never started again. It was pushed onto the transporter and went back to the factory."

MINNEY
Le Mans

"The 330LM was an absolute lump. A GTO was a superbly crafted machine, it looked the business and it did the business but the 330LM definitely was not one of Enzo Ferrari's better efforts. It didn't look particularly nice and it certainly was not better than the GTO in any way. I just couldn't get excited about it at all.

"It did have a nice gearbox in it, despite the fact that it didn't have any synchromesh, and it was a lovely car to drive. If cars were prepared at F. English we often used to stick trade plates on them and make sure they were running properly. When we changed axle ratios the car had to be tried before it went off to the circuit. So with trade plates on we'd go off and do a road test. That was part of the fun.

"I think the car was bought by Ronnie Hoare from the factory, it finished up in the UK and was driven by Bandini at Brands Hatch. As much as Enzo Ferrari liked his concessionaires I don't think he'd let them have cars to go racing with, then let them buy the cars afterwards. I think you had to give him a commitment on a purchase.

"We had gearbox problems with the car. It developed an oil leak and we decided that it was going to take too long to cure it. We knew where it was, on the extension shaft, so we decided to soldier on. We put an oil additive in the gearbox oil and it managed to stop it seizing up. Every pitstop that we could put oil in it we had to get the oil barrel out to top the gearbox up. But it stayed in one piece so it was a successful first trip to Le Mans."

GUICHET
Le Mans

"Our Ferrari was one of the 4.0 litre 330LMs which was lent to us against a deposit cheque to cover any damage. After five hours we were fourth overall when there was a cloud of smoke behind the car on the Hunaudieres straight and I lost twelve of the fifteen litres of oil from the tank. The oil filter had not been tightened properly at the previous pit stop. I drove the car slowly back to the pits.

"In accordance with the regulations we were not allowed to refill with oil because we had not covered enough distance. Dragoni asked me to go back onto the track and complete the required number of laps. Realising the risk to the engine I asked for my deposit cheque to be returned first. A wind of panic flew through the Ferrari pits and there was a lot of discussion. Someone even tried to call the Commendatore in Maranello for a decision.

"After all this was the cheque was not returned so the car stayed in the pits."

PIPER
Rheims French Grand Prix GT Race

"I had only one mechanic, Fairfax 'Fax' Dunn, and we did the best we could with our limited resources against the works team. The only way to be competitive was to develop the car. We would always tear a new car down and rebuild it with our own modifications.

"A new GTO would usually have an air cleaner and a long exhaust system so the first thing to be done would be to fit longer trumpets on the carburettors and an exhaust tuned for racing. We would also change things like brakes and some suspension parts. Some of our changes are still secret.

"The main change we made to the new GTO was to cut six inches off the roof pillars to reduce the frontal area, which was important on a circuit as fast as Rheims. It looked much better than the normal GTO, the roof line tapered down to the tail in a far nicer line. Forghieri and Bandini used to keep an eye on our car and would sometimes ask if I could get them some of the parts we had added to the car. They both said later that it was the fastest GTO in the world.

"Developing the car was part of the fun, I enjoyed that as much as driving."

MINNEY
Martini International Trophy, Silverstone

"During practice we found that the rainwater was going straight down through the brake scoops and getting on the pads, reducing the braking effectiveness by quite a large amount. So for the race we made some covers to close up the front scoops."

SEARS
Grovewood Trophy Mallory Park

"Mallory was a funny circuit, only two corners really mattered and acceleration out of the hairpin was all important. I made a good start and led into the first corner pulling away from Roy Salvadori and Graham Hill.

"Graham soon caught me and I could see why he had chosen the E Type for this race. The Jaguar had so much more torque out of the hairpin that he was gaining there every lap as he out accelerated me. Through Gerards and the Esses the GTO had far better handling and if you could get it right there you were on a very quick lap but Graham's acceleration out of Shaws decided the race."

Le Mans 1963: Gregory/Piper in NART's 4713GT, the only GTO fitted with the 330LM-type body. Here it leads the Beurlys/ Langlois GTO 4293 into Mulsanne corner. The NART car came home sixth overall.

SALMON
Grovewood Trophy Mallory Park

"It was such a Mickey Mouse circuit and the GTO was a car you had to learn and work at. With other types of cars if you took liberties you would lose it and spin off. But with the GTO you were just beginning to get the hang of it and the thing was going quicker and quicker through the corners.

"That is why the GTO Ferrari was such a huge success, because it handled like no other car at that time. It came from the fact that the engine was buried deep and very low in the chassis. It was in a class quite by itself, the most beautifully balanced GT car I've ever driven. It was literally a ballet dancer on four wheels, you could do anything with it.

"It didn't really have a lot of torque. It didn't even come on song until about 4000 revs, but it used to howl and shriek right up to the top end and you went through the corners sideways without a worry in the world."

SEARS
Guards Trophy Brands Hatch

"The first thing I noticed was that the John Coombs car handled exactly like the Maranello car that I'd driven before. In the race I had a real duel with Innes' Aston Martin. I knew the Aston had superior grunt and was quicker out of the slow corners but the GTO had vastly superior handling qualities, especially through the faster curves.

"We were very close for most of the race, fighting hard with Innes ahead. Two thirds of the way into the race going down through Dingle Dell I was right on the Aston's tail and got alongside at Stirlings. Innes was off line slightly and had to give way. I pulled away and finished fifth, winning the GT class".

SALVADORI
Coppa Inter Europa Monza

"The competition was going to be between the Astons and the GTOs. Bianchi was driving the other car. We had very little practice in the cars because it had been raining, so we didn't know quite how

we would shape up.

"Parkes was the fastest GTO. In the early laps I lost a few seconds to him but I started to catch him, then we had a very quick pitstop and I scored a few seconds and we were then lapping together. From then on for the last hour and three quarters of the race we changed position virtually every lap.

"It was a super comparison between the two cars. My brakes should have been vastly superior, we were going down to the braking points of the Formula One cars. A number of Formula One drivers were watching because they'd heard that there was a dice going on and were very interested.

"We were going way past the three hundred marker boards before braking with these very heavy cars. It was really quite incredible. The brakes seemed to be alight at times. But even then I didn't have much of an edge on Parkes. I'm quite sure he was braking with me. Monza was the only time I've ever known any car equal the Aston on brakes. For three hours our brakes didn't fade despite being used hard all the time.

"We just went quicker and quicker and quicker and I thought, 'This has got to stop somewhere'. We had

the same lap times but it just boiled down to him having more acceleration than me while I had a slight edge on maximum power. He had a five speed box whereas there was a four speed on the Aston and he could always nip past me going up to the line. He'd follow me closely into the long right hander before the pits but he could out accelerate me all the time and just nip by before the line and then I could overtake him at the end of the main straight because I had slightly more grunt.

"I knew that if we arrived together on the last lap Michael would win, he would get his nose in front over the line so I had to outfox him sometime. It was all nice and clean because it was potentially very dangerous swapping position on every lap.

"We were giving each other signals of what we intended to do. We nodded to each other when we were going to attempt to pass and if I thought that I didn't want him to go by I would just put my hand up to say, 'I'm going in, don't try to pass me'. Or I would point for him to the right, so that if he had the opportunity he would try to pass me on the right and I would expect it.

"I never discussed the race with Michael but I think

he may have thought that I was too confident and felt all the time that I could pull away from him, which I could not. He possibly thought, 'Well, Roy's telling me what to do so he must be pretty confident that he'll pull away towards the end and he's making it look good'. That wasn't the case at all. I knew I had to outfumble him passing cars. Once or twice I tried it by delaying my overtaking. Usually he would queue up with me and we would go through together.

"Two laps from the end we came up behind two cars in the Lesmo bends and I thought, 'It's touch and go whether I can get through.' At the last moment I thought, 'Christ, I'm going for it.' By this time Michael was caught off balance and I slammed through past both cars. He got past one but was closed out by the second and as he came out of the corner he got into a tremendous drift and went a little onto the dirt and had to lift his foot.

"On the lap that I lost him I made the fastest lap of the race, I got away by a second and a half and with only two laps to go I managed to keep that lead to the end of the race. If it hadn't been for those two cars I think the result would have been different. But that's what makes motor racing."

GUICHET
Tour de France

"In the two hour race at Rheims I was slipstreaming Schlesser's GTO until he had to pit to refuel but he was racing so hard that he overshot the pits and had to do another lap. After his stop he dashed back into the race and in trying to catch up over revved his engine and broke a valve spring. Slipstreaming him allowed me to finish the race without a refuelling stop and take the lead of the Tour.

"After our win at Rheims we had to have the vales reset and we lost a lot of time while it was done. To make up the lost time we had to drive flat out on the road section to Caen. According to my co-driver Jose Behra we covered the distance at an average speed of over 180 km./hr."

KERRISON
Tour de France

"We set off from Strasbourg at night and the first thing we did was a hillclimb. In order to keep awake I'd armed myself with those pills that used to keep fighter pilots awake during the war. The awful thing is that one became completely uninhibited and lost all fear. We went up this first hill in the dark and about half-way up we ran out of road and went into the sand on the outside of a corner. We dug the car out, got it back on the road again and we got to the top having still made third fastest time!

"There were about six or seven cars in the big GT class and we got together and decided it was really an awful nuisance stopping at all these checkpoints. There was one that was particularly difficult to find. So we decided that if none of us went through this checkpoint they couldn't disqualify the whole of the big class. So the whole lot of us went straight down the autobahn nose to tail at about a hundred and fifty and ignored it!"

GROSSMAN
Bridgehampton

"I got a ride in a car that wasn't mine. A guy who sponsored me by the name of McKelvy bought a GTO but it wasn't a very good car. I broke down somewhere on the track and I had to have assistance from another driver. He was working on his own car which had also stopped and I asked him to help, I'm not a mechanic at all and he fixed whatever was wrong with it.

"After the race McKelvy said, 'That's not a very good car is it?'

"I said, 'No. Will you sell me the car?'

"I always kept my cheque book with me at races because I'm a car dealer and one never knows what's gonna happen at a race. He agreed and I paid fifty five hundred for it, which is interesting in the light of what these cars are worth today."

1964

INTRODUCTION

Nurburgring 1000Kms. 1964: the Bianchi/ Langlois von Ophem GTO-64, chassis 5575GT, which finished fourth overall, second in Division III GT. Note that the bonnet is as yet without the air scoop.

For 1964 the GT Championship regulations underwent further modification. The capacity limits for the smaller Divisions were revised, making Division I for cars of up to 1300cc. while Division III went unchanged as over 2000cc. However, the classes within Division III were altered, to 2001 - 3000cc and over 3000cc. Further, guaranteeing bewilderment for all concerned, a new co-efficient system was introduced, along with a complex sliding scale of minimum weight according to engine capacity.

Le Mans was now the only event with a co-efficient of two or more, and was worth 18 points to the winner. While it had a co-efficient of 2.0, Sebring, the Targa Florio, the 'Ring and the Paris 1000Kms. races and the Tour de France each carried a co-efficient of 1.6, making victory worth 14.4 points. All other established circuit events had a co-efficient of 1.3 making victory worth 11.7 points while hillclimbs, rallies and any race event in the series for the first time had a co-efficient of 1.0. The minimum participation criteria of '63 were still applied.

The sliding scale of weights increased the minimum weight per 50cc. of engine capacity. Increments ranged from 10 kilogrammes per 50cc. from 500cc. - 1300cc. to 3.75kg. per 50cc. over 4000cc. with a ceiling of 1000kg.

The GT Prototype series was expanded with two further rounds, at Bridgehampton and Montlhery, making a total of six events.

To defend the GT series crown, Ferrari had to develop a revised GTO: the authorities would not budge on the question of the 250LM and the Cobra threat was growing. With both Porsche and Cobra playing to the homologation rules it was just that the 250LM should not yet be accepted as a GT: there existed but one example at the start of the '64 season. Having refused to sell his soul to Ford, Enzo Ferrari could not only huff and puff over the 250LM. He had to find the means to beat the Cobra on the track in the form of a carefully re-worked GTO.

Thus the GTO 64 was a straightforward development of the original. The engine had valve timing and carburation improvements resulting in no increase in power (from the established level of 296 - 302 b.h.p.) but in an improvement in the power band. Other than for appropriate gear ratio revisions, mechanically the '64 car followed its forerunner.

A reshaped bodyshell reminiscent in looks of the outlawed 250LM was devised by test driver Michael Parkes and Ingegnere Mauro Forghieri and was put into metal by the factory racing department rather than a sub-contractor. The cabin was almost identical to that of the 250LM, to the point where two of the GTO 64s were fitted with an aerofoil on the trailing edge of the roof while the others had a long roof configuration.

The wheelbase remained unaltered to ensure homologation as an evolution of the original but an increase in front track width to 1445mm. and rear track to 1414mm. with wider wheels was eventually permitted by the FIA.

Three brand new cars were constructed to GTO 64 specification while four of the earlier examples were sent back to the factory to be fitted with Scaglietti built bodywork and in some cases to receive the engine and wheel modifications.

The three new cars began their racing career with warm induction taking air from the flow passing through the elliptical radiator inlet. By Le Mans two of the three along with the converted Maranello Concessionaires car had been converted to cold air ram induction in a quest for top end power, this involving opening the leading edge of the carburettor bulge on the bonnet panel.

GTO RIVALS

Aston Martin's Le Mans hopes had been shattered in '63 with the DP215 and both DP214s retiring. In spite of Salvadori's fine win at Monza, stealing the Coppa Inter Europa from local hero Ferrari, the Aston Martin factory withdrew at the end of the season. The factory DP214 cars were sold to Michael Salmon and

Brian Hetreed and thus on paper remained a threat in the GT ranks. Britain's other representative, Jaguar built no new lightweight E Types but a number of E Type teams carried on the fight, in spite of a lack of success for the marque in 1963.

Logically, 1964 was GTO versus Cobra. Ford did not

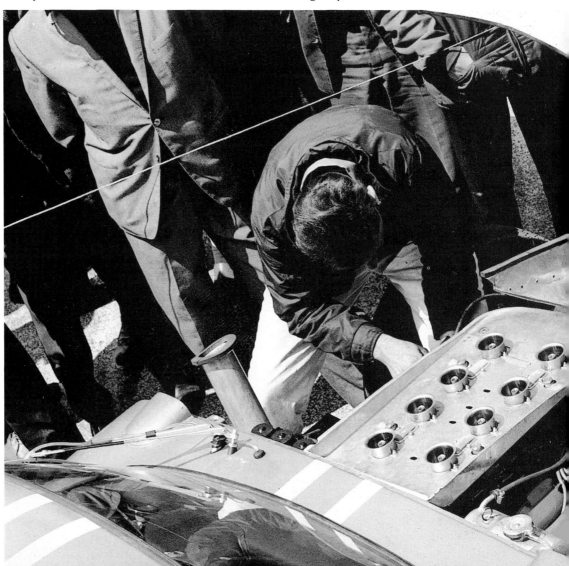

Le Mans 1964: a Shelby Daytona-bodied Cobra says 'Aah!' in the paddock prior to the 24 Hour race. That race saw the V8 Ford-engined machine bring to an end the Ferrari domination of GT at La Sarthe.

reduce its support for Shelby: on the contrary its racing programme was growing and '64 saw the debut of the GT40 Sports-Prototype. Legend has it that it was the shock of the Cobra defeat at Sebring in '63 that had led Henry Ford to try to buy out "those fast red cars". Certainly, between the Sebring defeat and the Bridgehampton success (against a much weaker Ferrari opposition) a Ford takeover of Ferrari had come close to reality. Quite why it fizzled out at the eleventh hour has never really been made clear.

The upshot was the development of the GT40 and backing for Shelby to make an all out attack on the GT crown with the Cobra. Shelby American Incorporated developed a new version of the Cobra - having already constructed 100 units. The standard Cobra chassis with 289 cubic inch Ford V8 had the radiator canted

forward and was reinforced with extra tubes which also supported a sleek new coupe body. Its shape was from the pen of Peter Brock, an ex-GM man who had worked on the '63 Corvette Stingray.

The nose and bonnet was dominated by a large forward radiator intake and an upward radiator exit ahead of the engine and the raked windscreen. The roofline sloped gently rearward terminating in the Kamm manner with a flat vertical panel. The new coupe bodies were constructed right in Ferrari's backyard at Carrozzeria Gran Sport in Modena. One version of a coupe body was made independently by the Alan Mann Racing operation in England, this slightly more bulbous.

GTO RACE RECORD

The 1964 season started with the Daytona Continental, a 2000 kms. race. Pedro Rodriguez and Phil Hill won in a new NART car, 5571, which had the '64 body shape. They lost time during a long pit stop to cut away damaged bodywork, after a blown tyre had pitched the car into the retaining wall on the banking. For a while the car ran with one headlight in the dark, until the team was ordered to fit another by the race organisers.

The early hours of the race were led by a 4.7 litre Cobra coupe, until its differential failed. Piper and Bianchi in 4491 finished second overall. The green car was in second place early in the race, but lost 29 minutes having the alternator replaced.

Norinder/Cannon took fifth in the Swedes' car, 3445, Perkins/Slottag in 3223 bought from Grossman by Perkins were eleventh. 3767 driven by Cantrell/Harry Heuer also rán, but there appears to be no record of what happened to this car. Grossman/Hansgen shared 4713 which had been bought by Grossman from NART, though was still entered by NART. They retired with electrical problems.

The "home" team got its revenge a few weeks later, on the flat and featureless Sebring airfield circuit, three Cobras finishing ahead of NART's Daytona winner, 5571, which was driven by Piper/Gammin. The latter was, however, substituted by Rodriguez when the Mexican's Ferrari prototype retired. The NART car was seventh overall at the finish.

Thompson/Grossman in the NART-entered 4713 were 15th and Perkins/Eve in 3223 27th ahead of Heuer/Yenko/ Cantrell in another GTO. 5573, another new GTO with the 64-type body, was disqualified for receiving outside assistance.

The British GT season commenced as usual with the Sussex Trophy at Goodwood. Graham Hill in Maranello Concessionaires 4399, which had been rebodied in the new style over the winter, won after being led for the first four laps by Sears in the John Willment Cobra. It was a close-run thing, the final margin of victory only 0.8 seconds.

The Sebring class win had dispelled any doubts over the wisdom of Shelby American embarking on an expensive, ambitious European programme. They could hardly have chosen a worse debut venue than the Targa Florio, but sure enough there was a brace of cars from the California GT builder in Sicily for the start of practice.

Ferrari took the challenge from America's Venice so seriously that for the first time it prepared and ran a works GTO in Division III. This was chassis 4675, the car crashed by Fossati/Francolino in the 1963 Tour de France and rebuilt as a GTO 64. For the Sicilian race it was entered under the banner of the Scuderia Sant Ambroeus to be driven by Guichet and Carlo Facetti.

Initially the plan worked, for 4675 led the big GT class by miles driven by Guichet, lowering the GTO Targa lap record by over a minute on the standing start lap, then by a further minute and a half on the first flying lap. Alas, co-driver Facetti brought the car in to retire on the fifth lap having ruined the gearbox due to inexperience. By half distance, with Ferrari not running any prototypes and the Porsche prototypes having broken, the works GTO had been looking for a good bet for overall honours, so it was a double disaster for Guichet and the factory.

The works GTO was backed up by five older, private entries, but none was driven with much verve. Thankfully for Ferrari, chassis breakages decimated the Cobra challenge. The race fell to Porsche's new Division II GT challenger, the 2.0 litre 904, two such factory-assisted cars and two factory Alfa Romeo Zagatos running in the same category (entered, ironically enough, by Sant Ambroeus) finishing ahead of the top GTO.

Although humbled, 3413, driven by Corrado Ferlaino and Luigi Taramazzo collected the valuable Division III points. This car was one of the first GTOs built which Ferlaino had bought from Bulgari. It had been rebodied in the '64 style but with a smooth roof without the spoiler on its trailing edge.

Norinder/Picko Troberg in 3445GT were ninth overall and second in class, Bourillot/de Bourbon Parme in the same car they had run in the '63 Targa finished tenth again, entered by Filipinetti, but the car now owned by Bourillot. 3705 finished thirteenth overall for the second successive year, Nicolosi shar-

ing his car entered by Scuderia San Marco with Zanardelli. "Ulysse"/Fortimbrass in 3647, bought by A. Bossa from Tchkotoua and rebuilt after Hitchcock's accident at the 1963 Goodwood TT, failed to finish.

The GT race at the International Trophy Meeting at Silverstone fell to Graham Hill in 4399 again. Hill won by 12.2 seconds on a wet track, Piper was third in 4491. Kerrison in 2735 was eleventh on the grid but did not feature.

From the Sicilian countryside, the World Championship battle moved to the high speed circuit at

1964

Francorchamps in Belgium for the 500 kms. race, which received entries for no less than eleven GTOs and two Drogo specials and saw Mike Parkes put Maranello Concessionaires' 4399 on pole. However, it wasn't the fastest car in the race; that honour went to Phil Hill's quick but troubled Cobra.

The 36-lap, 315-mile race was led at the start by Hill's Daytona coupe-bodied Cobra - as far as Stavelot on the first lap, where Parkes got by. Parkes led to finish: the Ford-powered car was seriously

delayed by a blocked fuel line.

Guichet in the ex-Targa factory car was second, ahead of Bandini in the ex-Sebring NART '64 car, and Piper fourth in 4491, despite a late pit stop to replace a damaged wheel. Langlois van Ophem was sixth in Dumay's Ecurie Francorchamps-entered 4153. Noblet took 13th in his own car, 3943, which was the last GTO to finish.

Manfred Ramminger in 4115, previously owned by H. Cordes and raced almost exclusively in Germany,

did not finish - neither did Norinder in 3445, Clarke in 5757 or Boulanger in 4757, an ex-SSR car owned by Ecurie Marquet and entered by Ecurie Francorchamps. Bianchi, driving Ecurie Francorchamps' brand-new 5575, blew a head gasket in its first race. Of the Drogo specials, Francis Van Lysbeth crashed and wrote off 2053, while Kerrison in 2753 had a universal joint break and retired.

The ADAC 1000 Kms. was another disastrous race for the Cobras, another field day for the GTO. The class win and second overall, due to a high mortality rate among the prototypes, fell to Guichet sharing 5573 with Parkes. Fourth overall and second in class but behind the 2.0 litre class winning Porsche was the Ecurie Francorchamps' car 5575, Bianchi sharing with Langlois van Ophem.

Two cars had languished as low as 56th at the end of the first lap of the Nurburgring, having been delayed by an accident which partially blocked the road. Piper, sharing with Cooper Formula One driver Tony Maggs, finished seventh in 4491; Van Lysbeth/Gustave Gosselin in Francorchamps 4153 were 18th, a lap behind the 1300c.c. class-winning Abarth. Ramminger/Schander in 4115 were 20th and Clarke/Margulies in 3757 were 28th. Norinder and young New Zealander Chris Amon sharing 3445 were the only GTO crew who, of the seven entered, failed to finish; an accident ended their race.

So, prior to the Le Mans classic, the World Championship score read: Ferrari four wins, Cobra one. Le Mans was a turning point for the American challenger. Not surprisingly, Ford's new and inadequately tested sports prototype failed to break Ferrari's stranglehold on the outright results. However, its now-racewise GT cousin dealt with the Italian marque a hefty blow.

Le Mans saw, as ever, the biggest GT battle of the year. Ferrari was represented by all three '64 cars, the factory machine 5571 running under the NART banner in the hands of Tavano/Grossman, alongside the Daytona winner 5571 handled by Hughes/Jose Rosinski. Ecurie Francorchamps' example was driven by Bianchi/Beurlys. The GTO ranks were completed by the Maranello Concessionaires Spa winner, which also had the 64 body shape, entrusted to Ireland/Maggs - Parkes having been drafted into the works' prototype team.

The principal opposition came in the shape of two Shelby coupes crewed by Gurney/Bondurant and Amon/Neerpasch, backed up by a conventional Cobra entered by the A.C. Car Company and driven by Sears/Bolton. In addition, there were three other competitive Division III runners which couldn't be overlooked - an Aston Martin for Salmon/Sutcliffe, lightweight Jaguar for Lumsden/Sargent and a special works E Type for Lindner/Nocker.

The strongest Division III runners quickly emerged as the Cobras of Gurney/Bondurant and Sears/Bolton. The factory Jaguar was a disappointment due to an imprudently low rear axle ratio, causing over-revving as the engine loosened after the first couple of hours, while the lightweight car suffered gearbox failure.

The Aston was, however, in great form, keeping the GTOs out of the top three positions. However, it didn't sustain the performance and was eventually disqualified for taking on oil. The second Shelby Cobra was also disqualified for a minor rule infringement during the night but the Gurney/Bondurant car remained the Division III pacesetter, slipping back only temporarily due to a leaking oil pipe.

While the pipe was fixed Tavano/Grossman moved into the class lead but they were forced to slow when, in their attempts to stay ahead of the American car, their GTO suffered two bent valves. The other GTOs weren't quite strong enough to combat the Cobra coupe.

Ireland/Maggs suffered intermittent clutch slip throughout, and Hughes/Rosinski were victims of a broken rear axle, retiring when the transmission seized on the start/finish straight, the casing spectacularly exploding and showering shrapnel into the spectator area and pits, where some hit a Jaguar being worked on by its mechanics.

At the finish the Bianchi/Beurlys car was the best-placed GTO, fifth overall, but a lap behind the class-winning Cobra. So near and yet so far. Ireland/Maggs slipped home sixth, while Tavano/Grossman fell to ninth, having to contend with a failing engine.

Back in England at the Martini International at Silverstone, Ferrari representative Kerrison in 2735 failed to finish.

From Le Mans the international action moved to the other side of Northern France for the fast Rheims Twelve Hour race in which the Cobra once again was a force to be reckoned with. The Cobra of Bondurant and Gurney was delayed with overheat-

Paying homage...

ing and finally went out with a broken gearbox casing, but the sister car of Ireland/Neerpasch took the class lead in the third hour, demoting Parkes/Scarfiotti in the usual Maranello Concessionaires' GTO, which had led in the early laps.

However, Ferrari fortunes improved at the five-hour mark when a leaking exhaust began to feed fumes into the Cobra's cockpit. It had to be repaired using parts from the Gurney/Bondurant car, costing half an hour and dropping the Daytona coupe out of all contention.

Parkes/Scarfiotti went on to take third overall and the GT class win, despite the Maranello car suffering a repeat of its Le Mans carburettor icing problem, which was solved by blocking part of the bonnet air scoop. Piper/Maggs in Piper's lowline '63 car, which suffered brake problems late in the race, were fourth. Rodriguez/Vaccarella in 5571 finished ninth, having had to cope with elusive brakes.

Norinder's old-style car (3445) was seriously delayed with electrical problems, despite the efforts of its notable driver pairing of Chris Amon and Ferrari debutant Jackie Stewart. The star of Formula Three in 1964, Scot Stewart was a late replacement for the

car's owner, who was getting married. The Swedish-owned car eventually took 17th place. Grossman was in the second NART car, 5573, sharing with the unfortunate Skip Hudson who was driving with a broken finger after it had been shut in a car door accidentally.

Interestingly, a 2.5 litre ATS GT finally appeared for Cabral and Zeccoli but non-started after being badly damaged when hit by another car, following its breaking down at the roadside during practice.

The Freiburg-Schauinsland hillclimb on August 9th again counted for the GT Championship and Scarfiotti in 5573GT won the three litre class of Division III in 6min.56.42s. Unlike the previous year, there was stiff opposition for the GTO, in the form of three Cobras which dominated the over 3.0 litre class, Bondurant winning from Neerpasch and Siffert. The Cobra's winning time of 6min.55.89s. gave maximum Division III points to Shelby American.

Between Rheims and the Goodwood TT there were a number of British Championship events. In the Ilford Films Trophy at the British Grand Prix Meeting at Brands Hatch, Piper was fourth in 4491 in a race won by the Cobra of Sears. Sears had been black-flagged for taking the wrong position on the starting grid, and had to overcome the delay of being hauled into the pits for admonishment from the clerk of the course.

At Snetterton in the race for the Scott Brown Trophy, Peter Clarke took sixth place in 3757. The race was won by Salvadori in a Maranello 250LM. In the Guards Trophy race for sports racing and GT cars at Brands Hatch, Ireland in 4399 retired with brake problems; Kerrison in 2735 went out of the race for the same reason.

Having been run exclusively for GT cars since 1960, the twenty-ninth Tourist Trophy Race, held at Goodwood again, was also open to sports prototypes which dominated the front of the grid. A heavy Cobra presence was indicative of how seriously Shelby American were taking things. Gurney's Daytona Coupe was fastest GT in practice, albeit only eleventh on the grid. Surtees was the fastest GTO driver in NART's 5573 in seventeenth.

On the ninth lap of the race Ireland in 4399 collided with one of the small capacity prototypes, causing other cars to spin. Surtees, following closely, hit one of them with sufficient force to flip over it, roll off the circuit and into the earth bank at St. Mary's. For the second time in three TTs, Surtees had made a violent exit.

The World Champion elect was taken to hospital with concussion. Ireland stopped at the pits to have bodywork damage rectified, the nearside front wheel arch needing to be beaten off the tyre. The GT category was dominated throughout by the Cobras, the first three places being Shelby American property for the whole race.

Ireland recovered to take sixth place as a number of leading contenders retired, although at post-race scrutineering the car was found to be wider than the measurement on its homologation certificate. It was initially awarded the place only provisionally, although sixth was subsequently officially confirmed.

Ginther in 3729, now owned by Viscount "Eddie" Portman but still entered by John Coombs, finished ninth, a last lap spin letting Lumsden's E Type past. Maggs in Piper's green car 4491 was tenth, delayed late in the race by a pit stop for a change of brake pads. The race was won by Graham Hill's Maranello Concessionaires' 330P.

On the following day the Sierre-Montana-Crans hillclimb saw another major Cobra effort, the Ford powered cars of Bondurant, Schlesser and Neerpasch filling the top three positions in the over 3.0 litre class of Division III, netting another maximum points score.

Pierre Sudan won the 3.0 litre class in GTO 3809 but was well short of the Cobra times. Putting the larger capacity cars to shame was the 2.0 litre class winning Abarth which was a minute ahead of Sudan and also beat Bondurant by two seconds, in spite of its 3.0 litre displacement deficit.

The 1964 Coppa Inter Europa race at Monza lost its championship status and became a mediocre affair compared to the previous year's thriller, and was notable mainly for Prinoths' accident in which 3851 was rolled and heavily damaged. Nicolosi in 3705 was fourth at the finish, ahead of Sigala in 4675 but behind a trio of 250LMs.

The 1964 Tour de France was billed as the big showdown between Ferrari and Shelby for the GT and World Manufacturers' Championship. Four Cobras lined up against eight GTOs. The first three stages were won by the American cars but, by the mid-point of the marathon event, all had retired, leaving the race and championship open for Ferrari.

Bianchi/Georges Berger in Ecurie Francorchamps 4153 battled for the lead with Guichet/de Bourbon Parme in Guichet's 5111GT, the former determined to take the win that had eluded him for the previous two years, the latter equally resolved to repeat his win of 1963.

Piper/Siffert in Maranello's 4399 were disqualified for unauthorised refuelling at Le Mans, where Tavano retired immediately after the race. He missed a gear in 5095 that he was sharing with Martin, and blew a piston.

In the final race at Monza, Guichet suffered brake failure and trailed home in sixth place, while Bianchi took a steady second place behind the eventual Ladies' Cup winners Annie Soisbault de Montaigu and Nicole Roure in Ecurie Francorchamps' 5575 GTO 64.

At the finish Bianchi/Berger were the winners ahead of Guichet/Bourbon Parme. Claude Dubois/Phillipe de Montaigu were eighth, with the latter's wife and her partner ninth. Langlois van Ophem/Gosselin in Ecurie Francorchamps' 4751 and Sylvain Garant/Jacques Lanners in Garant's ex-Tavano 3769 failed to make the finish.

The result secured the GT world title for Ferrari, despite there being two events left to run in the series. At the Bridgehampton Double 500 the only GTO entered blew its engine in practice and did not start. Inevitably, Cobras filled the first four places in the big GT class.

The last major race in Europe was the GT Championship finale, the Paris 1000kms. at the historic Montlhery circuit in the suburbs of Paris. Five GTOs were entered but there was no sign of the Cobras.

Rodriguez/Schlesser in NART's 5573 were second overall and first GT behind the 330P of Hill/Bonnier after mechanical problems eliminated many of the fancied prototype runners. Piper/Maggs were fourth in 4491, Piper wearing a body brace, a legacy of his accident in the Snetterton Autosport Three Hours in which he badly damaged his Ferrari 250LM.

Bianchi/Langlois van Ophem were fifth in 4153 and had been fastest GT in practice, ahead of even Rodriguez in the NART car. Eduardo Lualdi/Oddone Sigala were twelfth in 4091GT entered by Scuderia Sant Ambroeus, ahead of Gosselin/Dubois in 5575 which had a fraught race, at one stage being hit in the pits by Vaccarella's passing prototype while parked, having a split water hose replaced.

After the end of racing in Europe, David Piper took two cars to the Rand Nine Hours at Kyalami. 4491, driven by John Love/Pieter de Klerk, was second overall, de Klerk suffering burnt feet in the latter stages of the race. The GTO was six laps behind its owner and Maggs in a 250LM.

The year finished with the traditional Nassau TT in which Pedro Rodriguez was sixth, having mounted a strong challenge for the GT class, almost beating the Cobras until he had to stop to replace damaged wheels late in the race. Tom Fleming was eighth. The Nassau Trophy on the following weekend saw Phil Hill finish tenth to round off the GTO results in '64.

The 1964 GT Championship had been a tense battle between Ferrari and Cobra with the result in balance right up to the Tour de France. Right up until that point Shelby had retained a mathematical chance of achieving the unthinkable: defeating Ferrari in the GT category. In the event, the title went to Maranello by 84.4 points to 78.3 points.

Ferrari had called upon all its resources to repel the challenge of the Cobra in '64, including political shenanigans. The Coppa Inter Europa at Monza, an ideal circuit for the powerful Cobra, had been dropped after Ferrari - fearing home defeat - had refused to participate unless permitted to run the 250LM. The authorities had stood firm on the question of the 250LM, the race organisers had cancelled the event and out had gone a likely 11.7 points for Cobra...

At the end of '64 the FIA announced new regulations for the GT and GT Prototype classes. From '66 a minimum of 500 units would be required for homologation in the GT classes while only 50 would be required for a new Sports class to run alongside one-off Prototypes.

Tour de France 1964: the start of the Le Mans race. The GTOs of Bianchi/Berger and Guichet/de Bourbon Parme and the Trintigant/de Saint-Auban Shelby Cobra lead the field away on this stage.

BEHIND THE WHEEL

GROSSMAN
Daytona

"I was sharing with Hansgen and we were running third overall. The only problem we had was that one of the wire wheels was going to collapse. I knew it was going to happen in the bowl. Other than that we did alright. We were racing with Piper most of the way and finished third overall."

GROSSMAN
Sebring

"We did pretty well in that race until a strange thing happened. That race ended at ten o'clock in the evening and towards the finish the car started to run out of brakes. We found that it had a broken brake line and I had to come into the pits every half hour to replenish the brake fluid.

"Then there was a crash in front of the pits. A guy was looking for pit signals as he passed the hay bales and rammed the car in front causing a terrible fire that just about wiped out the pits. So I was unable to come in again to top up with fluid and had to drive the rest of the race with zero brakes. On an airport like Sebring that wasn't too easy."

DONALD McLEOD
Le Mans

"There was a hell of a mist down the Mulsanne straight and it was pretty cold. The car misfired going past the pits at about four o'clock in the morning, so we pulled it in and found that ice was forming on the top of the carburettors. We were literally chopping it out with screwdrivers. That was the only time we had any problems with that car.

"Gregor Grant of Autosport timed its pitstop and for the whole of the twenty-four hours it was in for only thirty-five minutes and about thirty seconds. All we did to it was change brake pads and tyres and fill it up with fuel.

"Of course, unlike today you didn't have a tank on either side and at Le Mans in those days you had to have the filler cap wired shut and marked with a seal. The trick was not just how fast you could get the fuel in, if you didn't keep in with the plombard he might walk away from the car and until he had sealed the tank you were not allowed out of the pits.

"Ronnie had decided that we should keep the pit officials very happy at Le Mans with wine and food. It did make a hell of a difference. After we had got our plombard tamed he would be standing waiting. As soon as we slapped the filler cap down he'd put the wire through and seal it and we'd be off.

"The only safety precautions we took when handling fuel in those days was that we wore gym shoes for better grip. We did wear overalls but they weren't flameproof by any means. At Le Mans there was a central fuel supply with a large hose in each pit but at other races we had to rely on churns and a big funnel. At races where we needed to refuel from churns, such as Goodwood, we got a really hefty chap about six foot six to pour the petrol in."

MINNEY
Le Mans

"Because mumblings were being made about the performance of the car the factory produced some new exhaust manifolds and new extractor pipes for the car. At the same time this was done they also put a new bonnet on to try to get more ram air down into the carburettors.

"My guess is that they realised that because of the change to the body shape hadn't really worked, they

*Le Mans 1964: GTO-64 chassis 4399GT driven by Innes
Ireland and Tony Maggs. This car came home sixth overall,
in spite of having effectively had no brakes for the final six
hours of the race.*

had to do something with the car. Rather than do the body again they probably felt that some new exhausts and the carburettor scoop might do the trick. They had tried side exhausts on a couple of the old shape GTOs but I don't think it really made a great difference.

"In the race it took two or three laps to realise that the carburettors were icing. We initially thought it was because Shell hadn't put any anti-ice content in the fuel. Either way we couldn't actually do much about it. We got the car in and I cut a hole in the bonnet with a hammer and a screwdriver and bent the metal up which allowed the hot air from the radiator to come out and also partially blanked off the cold air going directly into the intake on the carburettors.

"On Sunday Innes and Tony Maggs were both complaining about the brakes. They were saying that the pedal was a bit soft but it wasn't causing too much of a hassle. We checked it and found the pads were OK, there was plenty of fluid in and that there were no leaks in the system so they soldiered on.

"When the car came in immediately after the end of the race, it hadn't been stopped for long when I had to move the car. I put one foot on the brake pedal and it stopped two centimetres from the floorboard. I had to pump it to restore any pressure, the car had no brakes at all. So I got hold of Innes and said, 'Were the brakes like this when you were driving?'

'Oh yes,' he said, 'they've been like that for about six hours'."

GROSSMAN
Le Mans

"When the bent valves were suspected Chinetti wanted to withdraw the car and I wouldn't let him. He was tugging the car one way and I was tugging it the other. I felt we could finish the race and it was important to me because I had finished every Le Mans I had entered. It would have been my fifth finish and I wanted to maintain my record. So eventually he said, 'Alright, go ahead but don't go over 5000 r.p.m.'. So we continued from that point on at 4500-5000 r.p.m."

McLEOD
Rheims 12 Hours

"After Le Mans the car went back to the factory to be rebuilt before Rheims. When it came back we couldn't

find any sign of anything having been done to it. When Rob Chubb and I tackled Forghieri he said, 'We changed the clutch.' So that car ran practice at Le Mans, twenty-four hours in the race, practice at Rheims and twelve hours in the race with no engine rebuild and finished well in both events."

MINNEY
Rheims 12 Hours

"Maranello Concessionaires received a bill for repairs being carried out on the vehicle when it was brought to Rheims in the factory transporter. I clearly remember Ronnie Hoare asking for a report as to what we felt had been carried out. Obviously there's a limit to what you can report, you can't look inside unless you take the cylinder heads off, but you get to know the cars well enough to be able to see when things have been disturbed.

Rheims 12 Hours 1964: the NART GTO-64 chassis 5573GT driven by Grossman/Hudson leads the Maranello car, chassis 4399GT, driven by Parkes/Scarfiotti. Both cars suffered carburettor icing after dark.

Tour de France 1964: the GTO-64 driven by David Piper and Jo Siffert at speed on the Rouen-les-Essarts circuit. This car was highly competitive but was later disqualified for unauthorised refuelling.

Nino Vaccarella

"I helped Ron Chubb check the car over and I remember him reporting to Ronnie Hoare that he couldn't see that anything had been done to the car. In the race I remember it was really hot, and one of the most difficult and hard races the cars and team had done. It was very tiring."

NINO VACCARELLA
Rheims 12 Hours

"Our race was doomed from the start, a lengthy delay was forced on me by a brake pipe leaking fluid. I joined the race in thirty fourth place making it an uphill battle the whole way. Parkes and Scarfiotti came first in the Gran Turismo category while myself and Rodriguez came eleventh overall. All told it was a real shame since without the initial delay we could have realistically achieved third place outright and won the GT category. In any case the unexceptional result was still preferable to retiring."

GROSSMAN
Rheims 12 Hours

"We hadn't had the problems that the other GTOs had had at Le Mans but our carburettors iced up during the night at Rheims and then the gearbox broke. My co-driver Skip Hudson had broken his finger when he shut it in the door of his Peugeot hire car."

IRELAND
Tourist Trophy

"I think it happened somewhere around the back of the circuit. I was just ahead of Surtees and I thought the car ahead was giving me room to pass. I went to go inside him through Fordwater, which was taken flat out, but he obviously hadn't seen me and came in. I put a couple of wheels on the grass but still clipped him and I think I may have bounced this little fellow in front of Surtees."

SWATERS
Tour de France

"At the last race at Monza the Commendatore came to watch. He was always very keen when he saw a nice woman and we had Annie Soisbault driving one of our

1964

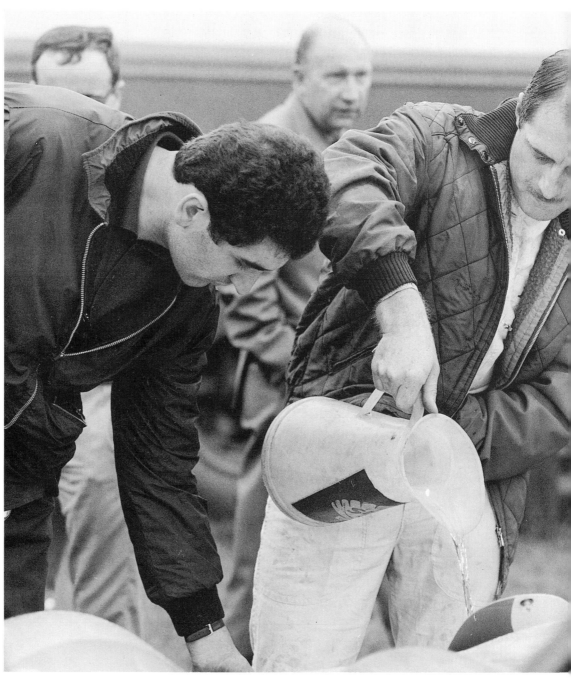

cars. Her husband, Phillipe de Montaigu, was one of the main financial backers of Ecuire Francorchamps at the time, a real enthusiast. He also wanted himself and his wife to drive but that was a bit of a problem for me. So for that Tour de France I entered four cars.

"By Monza we were in the lead of the Tour with Lucien Bianchi ahead of Guichet in second. During the race Guichet had a problem with his brakes and Lucien took the lead ahead of Annie Soisbault. I had a signal on the pit board telling Lucien to go slower. I gave him the same signal lap after lap but he was still a minute ahead of Annie. Finally he stopped at the pits

MINNEY
Tour de France

"The car had been prepared by the Assistanze and they had done a similar job to that done on Michael Parkes' car for the TT in 1962 and replaced just about everything in sight. The Tour de France was a long gruelling event but the car just wouldn't go. David knew GTOs exceptionally well but neither he nor a real charger like Seppi could get it to go. I think they had just replaced so many components on the engine to make sure it had finished the Tour in the first place, which I think it would have done.

"It was just beginning to loosen up. It was using a terrific amount of fuel. We knew the jet and the float levels were OK because I had checked it all out. It was just tight because of all the internal components that had been changed.

"We were on the starting grid at Le Mans and the Colonel thought we were allowed to top up with fuel having completed the warming up laps. As it turned out this was incorrect and we were immediately disqualified for an infringement of the regulations. It was a great pity because I felt very confident that we could have won.

"David was so consistent and gentle with the car, so too was Seppi, but he also had that extra sparkle that you needed when the pressure was on. The combination of the two in a Ferrari GTO was just right to get us onto the winners podium."

GUICHET
Tour de France

"The Ferrari I drove was the same car in which I had won the previous year. Unfortunately it had not gone through an overhaul before the 1964 Tour de France.

"Before the start of the two hour race at Rheims the engine was running very badly. In accordance with the rules we were not allowed to work on the car until after the race had started. After the start we changed all twelve spark plugs and our problem was cured. The delay cost us seventeen minutes which became a handicap on every day of the event and made a second win in two years impossible.

"In the final race at Monza a rear brake pipe broke. Florini hammered it flat to enable us to continue but we were beaten overall by Bianchi."

and asked me, 'Why do you keep asking me to go slow. I cannot go any slower than I am going.'

"When I told him he must let Annie Soisbault past, Lucien was not very pleased but the Commendatore was so happy to see a woman win at Monza in a GTO."

1964

KERRISON
Portuguese Grand Prix

"I picked up the GTO from Nice airport and I drove it on the road down through Spain to Portugal. I was somewhere in the middle of Spain at night and driving down a straight tree lined road at a comfortable ninety miles an hour, no traffic around at all when suddenly I had the impression of having driven into a lake.

"The car came to a stop and I realised that I was still alive. What had actually happened was that the road had flooded to a depth of about a foot. I'd just driven into this flood without perceiving that I was doing so until it was too late.

"When I tried to turn the engine over to get out of the lake, not unnaturally it wouldn't start. The water had of course gone up the nose of the car into the air scoop and filled the carburettor trumpets. So I opened the bonnet and there were the twelve Webers full of water. Even to someone as non-mechanical as myself it was obvious that was not right. So I baled them out with my handkerchief.

"It was quite remarkable because after about a minute of attempting to start the engine again it came back on, starting first on one, then two, then three, four, five, six until gradually all the cylinders started to fire, I had got it back onto twelve.

"After that incident the car wasn't touched before I ran it in the Portuguese Grand Prix and I won the race. I don't think many racing engines would put up with that kind of treatment."

SALMON
Portuguese Grand Prix

"It was a dream weekend which went very badly wrong. Christopher took two Ferraris out for the race at Cascais. He was to drive his Drogo bodied car and I was to race a lefthand drive 250GTO.

"I flew out from Heathrow late one night and there was Christopher waiting at the airport in the GTO. It was a beautiful hot, wonderful summer's evening. We practiced with both cars on a fascinating circuit. Of course, both cars were far quicker than anything else there but sadly Christopher's Drogo blew up in a big way. Dropped a valve or broke a piston or something, clouds of smoke belched out of it and that was that.

"I obviously felt embarrassed that he wasn't going to

drive when he owned both cars. So I said to him, 'Look Christopher this is not fair, you've been very kind to invite me to drive your car but now you haven't got a car to race, it's not right and not proper'.

"He said, 'Don't be silly Michael, what we'll do is share the driving'. It was quite a long race and we agreed to do 50/50. Unfortunately, I went down with some extraordinary bug and actually thought I'd got mumps, but I had a high temperature and felt absolutely frightful with a terrible stiff neck. I said, 'Look Christopher I honestly think I ought to go home because I'm feeling bloody awful and I don't want to be stranded in Lisbon, ill for a week or a fortnight'.

"So I caught the plane and flew home and he won the race in the car that I was supposed to be driving."

KERRISON
Mount Etna Hillclimb

"There was a motley collection of cars entered. I think I may have been the only Ferrari but there was everything there down to a Fiat Topolino. I drove the car by road all the way to Sicily.

"Going down the road north of Rome there was a group of a lorry and twelve cars ahead and it was perfectly apparent that any normal car could not conceivably undertake such an overtaking manoeuvre. When I pulled out the oncoming car which was about half a mile away immediately started flashing its lights as it was also going very fast. But I was round the twelve cars and the lorry and back on my side of the road again so quickly that it was still nearly half a mile away.

"When the other driver saw what had happened he drew a large breath and when he was where the car was he took both hands off the steering wheel and blew kisses. Driving through Sicily people leant out of windows and cheered as I went by. It seems that the further south you go in Italy the more seriously they take their motor cars. They're very hot blooded and very car minded."

HILL
Nassau

"All you had to do at Nassau was go off the road into this innocent looking grass. Buried in the grass was the most awful coral rocks you ever saw. It was the kind of stuff that would just rip the underneath of a car off so fast you wouldn't believe it."

Post '64

GTO RACE RECORD

Ferrari did not support the 1965 GT World Championship in the face of continuing refusal by the FIA to homologate the 250LM and, initially, the 275GTB, one hundred examples still lacking. Perhaps proving the evenhandedness of the governing body, Shelby's 1965 secret weapon, a 7.0 litre Cobra was also refused papers, but in the light of Ferrari's withdrawal it was unnecessary in any case.

The GTO was not modified for '65 but there were privateers who continued to campaign the existing examples, occasionally upsetting the Cobra steamroller. Realistically, by '65 the GTO epoch was over and the Cobra was the dominant force.

The season opener at Daytona attracted a single GTO, 3757 entered by Peter Clarke for himself/Bob Hurt/Charlie Hayes. They finished a creditable seventh overall, 19 laps down on the winner and fifth in class behind a quartet of Cobras. The GTO had been repaired after Clarke's shunt at a Goodwood club meeting the previous autumn.

In the Sebring 12 Hours the same car was entered for Clarke/Hurt but retired with clutch failure.

For the Sussex Trophy at Goodwood there were a pair of familiar cars running for the first time in new hands. Michael Salmon was in 4399, now owned by the Dawnay Racing team, while Peter Sutcliffe was in 4491 which he had bought from David Piper. The two GTOs set equal fastest time in practice but were beaten in the race by Roger Mac in a Chequered Flag Cobra roadster and Sears in a Willment Cobra Coupe. Sutcliffe spun early in the race but recovered to finish third ahead of Salmon.

In the GT class at the inaugural Monza 1000kms. run on the combined road circuit and high-speed banking, Cobras finished first and second ahead of Nember/ Bonomi in 4675. The GTO was eleventh overall, 12 laps down on the winner. Scuderia Filipinetti's 3527 shared by Boller/Spoerry was withdrawn after the team's prototype Ferrari crashed during the race, claiming the life of the promising young Swiss driver Tommy Spychiger.

The British season continued with the Tourist Trophy which had undergone a number of changes. The date was May and the race moved north to Oulton Park in Cheshire. A two-part race of two-hour heats was run with aggregate times to decide the final positions.

Salmon and Sutcliffe were beaten by Sears and Mac in practice but, in the first race, Sutcliffe finished sixth overall and won the GT class from Frank Gardner, Sir John Whitmore and Allen Grant in Cobras. Salmon retired with a broken brake pipe. In the second race Salmon was fourth overall, beaten by Sears' Cobra with Sutcliffe seventh behind Whitmore. The GT class was won on aggregate by Whitmore, who took fourth place in the final standings ahead of Sutcliffe. Salmon was unable to overcome his first heat handicap and was twelfth on aggregate.

The Targa Florio was always going to be the GTO's best chance for a class win in 1965. Of the four entered, Bourillot/Bourbon Parme in 4675 crashed, while Ravetto/Starabba finished twelfth overall and first in the GT class. However, they were almost beaten by the unlikely combination of Paul Hawkins and rally ace Timo Makinen in an Austin Healey 3000: the rotor arm broke on the British car.

Chassis 3647 of "Ulisse"/Marchesi and 3765LM of Pugacioff/Capuano both failed to finish. The latter chassis was one of the three 4.0 litre GTOs built in 1962 which had been fitted with a 3.0 litre Testa Rossa 250 engine in 1964, after being purchased from the factory.

Up in the Ardennes at the Spa 500kms., Sutcliffe finished fourth overall and first in the large GT category after two Cobras running in front hit trouble. Salmon was sixth on the road and third in class, beaten by Bondurant's Daytona Cobra, which was also closing fast on Sutcliffe at the finish. The home team Ecurie Francorchamps had a miserable day, Bianchi in 4757 non-starting and Langlois van Ophem in 4153 failing to finish.

Across the German border for the ADAC 1000kms. at the Nurburgring, Sutcliffe, sharing with Peter Lumsden, overcame the absence of a clutch and finished fifteenth overall and fifth in class behind three Cobras and the newly homologated Ferrari 275 GTB. Salmon/Kerrison retired 4399 with a broken half shaft. In 4115, Werner Lindermann/Manfred Raminger finished twenty-third; Clarke/Rollo Fielding did not finish.

There were no GTOs at Le Mans in 1965 but the Cobras were beaten to the GT class honours by a single Ferrari, an Ecurie Francorchamps entered 275GTB.

The Rossfeld Hill Climb resulted in a 1-2 for the Cobras, Bo Ljungfeldt in an Alan Mann-entered roadster setting best GT time.

At the Circuito de Mugello, a race run on some of the public roads that were used for the Mille Miglia in its heyday, Ravetto/Starabba in the sole GTO 4091 were deserted by their Targa Florio luck and failed to finish.

The Rheims 12 Hours was a similarly fruitless occasion for the GTO. Sutcliffe/Bill Bradley in 4491

Oulton Park Tourist Trophy 1965: Salmon in action in the ex-Maranello GTO-64, chassis 4399GT now run by Dawnay Racing. He finished fourth overall in the second leg but had retired from the first.

*Targa Florio 1965:
Ulysse/Marchesi in
3647GT. This was the
Bowmaker car of '62,
which had passed
through the hands of
Prince Tchkotova to A.
Bossa who ran it in the
'64 and '65 Targas
without success.*

retired with broken steering, Clarke/Fielding were stranded at the start with starter motor failure and Allen Grant/Guy Ligier in Ecurie Francorchamps' 4153 retired with a broken engine, leaving the GT class as a clean sweep for the Cobras.

The next round of the championship was the Ollon Villars hillclimb in Switzerland. Division III was won by Kocher in 3705, his time in the 3.0 litre class quicker than that of the unlimited class winner, Zwimpfer in a Ferrari 275GTB.

A new event for the series followed, the Coppa Citta di Enna, a 500 kms. thrash round the Enna Pergusa circuit which encircled a snake-infested lake. Bondurant and Sears finished third and fourth in the Alan Mann Cobras, winning the GT class. Latteri was fifth in 3765LM, as raced in the Targa Florio in May, ahead of Ravetto in sixth place in 4091.

The final race of the championship at Bridgehampton attracted no GTOs as the Cobras celebrated their World Title.

In 1966 the GT class was clearly on its way out. The category was contested by amateur drivers as the factory teams concentrated on the prototype categories which were now exclusively deciding World Championship honours.

There were still a small number of GTOs active, however. At the Daytona 24 hour Continental, the original GTO 3223, driven by Perkins/Slottag, finished nineteenth. Then it was badly damaged at the Sebring 12 Hours in a big accident.

In Italy at the Monza 1000kms. 4675 with Taramazzo/Giorgio Pianta driving did not finish; on the Targa Florio Marsala was involved in an accident with Bandini's Ferrari 330 P3 prototype but escaped lightly enough to give the factory driver a lift back to the pits!

The GTO bowed out of international competition in some style at the 1966 Paris 1000kms. at Montlhery. Chassis 3943, which had been mainly rallied previously, finished third overall in the hands of Robert Neyret/Jacques Teramorsi, two dentists from Grenoble! A big shunt on the first lap had delayed a number of faster cars, but it was a fine result nonetheless.

BEHIND THE WHEEL

Spa 500Kms. 1965: Sutcliffe at Francorchamps' daunting Eau Rouge corner. At this meeting the lowline ex-Piper GTO proved faster in a straight line than the '64-bodied car of Salmon/Bianchi.

Spa 500Kms. 1965: Michael Salmon in GTO-64 chassis 4399GT. In spite of problems with collapsing wheels, the English driver managed to finish sixth overall, third in Division IIIGT.

HAYES
1965 Daytona 200 Kilometres

"The GTO was very enjoyable on the banking at Daytona. The car would easily do the banking without lifting. We were running sixth at one stage with five sick prototypes ahead of us but I think we had some electrical problems otherwise we may very well have won, we certainly would have won the GT category.

"That GTO was a very nice car, in fact it was so quick I was suspicious that it might have had a 275 engine in it! I didn't voice my suspicion but it did seem to be an extraordinarily quick GTO."

PETER SUTCLIFFE
1965 Goodwood Sussex Trophy

"I was leading when I spun at Madgwick and rejoined at the back of the field. I think I was probably just going too fast. I passed Roger Mac at the beginning of that lap between the chicane and the next corner. I finished up third."

SUTCLIFFE
1965 Tourist Trophy Oulton Park

"If I'd known I could have won the whole GT category, I think I would have done so. I wasn't in any particular hurry in the second heat, the significance of beating them all in the first heat probably didn't occur to me in terms of the World Championship.

"Having won the up to three litre class I was quite happy, but with a little extra effort I could have won GT outright. There wasn't much difference in the times between my Ferrari and the Cobras so it wouldn't have been too difficult to consolidate the lead from the first heat."

SALMON
1965 Tourist Trophy

"Unlike people do today, I never at any time used to take the car for private testing. I would just go and practice in the allotted time and race. But on this occasion there was a day set aside prior to the official practice. Maranello brought the car up in their transporter with Ronnie Hoare's mechanics and I set about really getting to grips with it. In the first few laps I realised we were off the pace but I worked at it really hard that day, got the hang of it and it went extremely well.

"The TT that year was split into two parts and the brakes failed half way through the first part. I was fairly depressed about the situation because in order to stop going into the lake or running right off the road I had to go down through the gearbox and the rev counter tell-tale was up to nearly nine thousand. So I came in and the mechanics found that the brake pipe going to one of the rear calipers had fractured and so we withdrew the car and repaired the brake pipe during the interval.

"I remember Michael Parkes was a spectator there, he came up and asked if there were any problems. I said, 'Well, I don't think there's any point in starting the second half because I'm sure I've bent the valves.' He asked, 'Why?' and I told him about the brake failure and said, 'Look at the rev counter.' He shrieked with laughter and said, 'My dear Michael, you haven't got a problem, these engines are perfectly alright up to 9000 revs.'

"So we changed the plugs, fixed the brakes, got it ready and ran in the second half. Towards the end of the race I was furious with some little car that wouldn't get out of the way and I shook my left fist out of the window. When I came in at the end of the race I discovered that my rather nice gold watch had disappeared.

"Apparently a marshal saw it flying out of the window at 130 m.p.h. and picked up the remains and brought it into the paddock. I thought it had fallen off in the car so by that time we had all the seats out, but there it was, a sort of mangled mess having been picked off the track."

RICHARD BIRKS
1965 Spa Grand Prix

"We were running about fourth when Mike brought the car in and said that the thing was sliding around

all over the place. We changed the wheels and found that the spokes had actually collapsed. It was around that time that Dunlop had started spot coding their tyres and we were running white spot tyres that day, which were a new development. Up until that time Dunlop didn't really have a wet weather or dry weather tyre.

"They had just started producing these wider tyres which were all treaded but the actual rubber itself was softer for wet weather. White spots were dry weather tyres and green spots were wet weather tyres. The white spots we were using then had so much grip that the wheels just simply couldn't take it and collapsed, although not actually to the point where the car rode over the hub, but we broke them in practice and again in the race.

"We had them repaired by a man in Shepherds Bush, his business was called Motor Vehicle Repair Services but everyone knew him affectionately as Wire Wheel Willy. He used to repair all our Borrani wheels for us, going right back to the days when we were running DB3S's. He was the only man doing them."

SALMON
1965 Spa Grand Prix

"The 64 GTO was a bit disappointing in a straight line. There had been quite a few suggestions by Ronnie Hoare when Maranello had the car that it's engine performance wasn't up to scratch. Nobody ever really established whether that was the case or whether it was the new body design on the 64 shape that was actually aerodynamically not as good as the original shape. I remember storming down the Masta straight and Sutcliffe, who had the ex-Piper car with the lowered roof, just going straight past when we were both absolutely flat out without much difficulty at all.

"About five or six laps from the end we had a left-hand rear wheel collapse. We were running with the latest Dunlop tyres and they were beginning to produce problems with spoked wheels. The wheels had been rebuilt before we went out to Spa and when I came into the pits we had only six or seven spokes remaining in the left-hand rear wheel, which was causing all sorts of problems, but we managed to finish sixth.

"The wheels were flown back from Spa to Wire Wheel Willy in London and because the Nurburgring was the following week, we moved the car straight on to the Ring by road and the wheels were flown back to Germany before the race."

SUTCLIFFE
1965 Spa Grand Prix

"My fastest lap was 4.06 which was also the fastest that any of the Cobras did at any time. It was a very good race towards the end. I was again consolidating my lead in the three litre class and saw the Cobras coming up on me at the end. The last two laps were the fastest I drove in the race and matched

the time I'd done in practice and that was why I was able to stay ahead at the finish although there wasn't much in it over the line."

SUTCLIFFE
1965 ADAC 1000 Kilometres

"I had a collapsed rear wheel in practice so Ronnie Hoare lent me some others for the race which is why it had some silver wheels and some red. When I bought the car it was in David Piper's bright BP sort of green and I had it resprayed into my own racing green which was a dark metallic shade and the wheels were done red then. In retrospect, it wasn't all that attractive with red wheels, it looked a bit Indian.

"In the race we didn't really have any trouble apart from the clutch which stopped disengaging because Peter Lumsden had been driving with his foot on the pedal and it had just become terribly overheated. By the end, when I had taken the car over and driven for three or four laps without using the clutch at all it had cooled off and was perfectly alright. It was a temporary fault, I don't remember it slowing me down really."

SALMON
1965 ADAC 1000 Kilometres

"I was fairly irritated because the mechanics had dropped the front of the car off its racing jacks whilst changing the axle ratio and had dented the nose quite badly. I remember having a blinding row with them, saying, 'If I can race the car all over the place and not put a scratch on it, I think it's a bit unreasonable for you people to damage it while it's sitting in the garage.'

"So we went to the Nurburgring but instead of working on the car they went off to see the Queen Mother who was visiting Bonn. When they got back I said to Richard Birks, who was our senior mechanic, 'You've always said you've wanted to go round the circuit, now is your chance. Hop in and I'll take you.' I took him round absolutely flat out. He got out shaking and very white and we had no more trouble again... ever.

"I was sharing the car with Christopher Kerrison and we had a lot of problems with it in practice. The top link of the front left shock absorber broke and we had trouble with the fuel pumps, but eventually we got it going well.

"It was a Le Mans start, which was always a bit daunting, particularly so at the Ring because you didn't have much opportunity in those type of starts to get the seatbelts done up. So we taped the harness to the roof and round the back of the pits on the opening lap I was able to jam the steering wheel with my knees and get the lap strap done up. Once I'd managed that, the shoulder straps were easy to click in and I felt a million dollars.

"Psychologically, if you've got the seatbelts done up on the Nurburgring you just fly. The car went superbly well and we led the class. I came in and handed over a thirty-second lead to Christopher, having had no problems. Christopher maintained position through his stint and when he brought the car in I said to Richard at the pitstop, 'Let's just have a quick look at the spokes on the wheels, because we could have a problem.'

"Christopher also said that the brakes were getting very bad, the pedal was going down to the boards. Richard came back and said, 'On the left-hand rear wheel you've got three spokes snapped.' So they took the wheel off and as they did the end of the halfshaft fell out onto the track. The only thing that had been keeping the wheel on was the disc which had worn half the brake caliper away. So there was nothing for it but to withdraw the car."

BIRKS
1965 ADAC 1000 Kilometres

"We changed the axle ratio on the car overnight which was an evil job on a GTO. You had to take the oil tank out and pull it all out of the side. It was about a ten hour job altogether. Mike was right, he very rarely marked a car but unfortunately we did on that occasion.

"We had the car up on two cantilever jacks with all four wheels off the ground. When we changed the weight by lifting the axle out of the back, the front jack popped up in the air which marked the nose of the car. Normally we used to lay a couple of wheels on the jack to hold it down but on that occasion we didn't.

"I shall never forget being driven round the Ring, it was extremely impressive and bloody frightening. We went round in just under ten minutes, which in those days was pretty quick. I don't think he did it out of

any form of spite or to quell a mutiny within the crew, Michael created his own mutinies! But seriously, he drove impeccably and it's certainly something I shall remember to the end of my days.

"In the race we broke the end off the drive shaft. When we took the rear wheel off, the end of the half shaft was just laying there inside the hub. The reason for the breakage was simply that the hub nut wasn't done up tight enough. It was supposed to be tightened to 220 lb/ft but I think we only did it up to about 180 lb/ft and that was enough to cause the end of the shaft to break.

"We were never really told what the actual tightening torque should be. Ron Chubb, who was a big mate of mine from Maranello showed me initially how to change the axles and ratios and things like that and they were always done up just bloody tight. Of course there's tight and bloody tight, 180 lb/ft is bloody tight but they had to be tighter than that."

SUTCLIFFE
1965 Rheims 12 Hours

"The ignition and starter switch had expired so we had to start it after every fuel stop by getting underneath and shorting the starter across with a spanner. I still have the burnt, scarred spanner that John Pearson used to do that.

"Later the drop arm from the steering box sheared going round the righthand corner at the end of the straight which was extremely lucky. I just coasted into the side of the road and brushed the nearside headlight and mudguard against the *fracines* on the outside of the corner. That was the last time I raced the GTO. I got my Ford GT40 after that. Rheims was always intended to be my last with the Ferrari.

"I advertised it for three thousand pounds later in the year and never even got a reply. I tried to sell the car for four or five years but nobody would even make me an offer for it. In the end I sent it out to South Africa because some people I knew out there said they would buy it if I sent it out but they didn't. I went out to South Africa at the end of 1967 and converted it into a road car. I put it back to its proper roof configuration and put a proper screen in and a bit of trim inside and ran as a road car for years. At the end of the Seventies I sold it back to David Piper."

THE GTO AND
ITS RIVALS

FERRARI 250 GTO
INNES IRELAND

"I must say I liked the GTO as a car to race because it didn't do anything funny. Although it had a tendency to understeer as its first basic move, you could sense what it was doing and it was never vicious or nasty, you just gave it a bit of correction and lots of power and off it would go.

"It had a wonderful, wonderful engine, which pulled from quite low down and revved so effortlessly. The power was delivered nice and smoothly. However, it didn't have rack and pinion steering the gearing was a bit on the low side so you didn't get an awful lot of feel back through the steering but that was how Ferrari made their steering boxes at that time. Also, the brakes weren't a strong point, I seem to remember that you had to be a bit bloody careful with them. By and large they were very reliable cars.

"I used to take 3505 home quite often and drive it to the races I was taking part in. I remember driving it down to Brands Hatch on the road, when I arrived the mechanics put a hot set of plugs in it and changed the wheels and I drove it in the race, then drove it home again. My wife used to use it to go shopping, it was a very docile animal.

"The GTO was a very hot car to drive. On the car that I raced in America - 3589 owned by Tom O'Connor of Rosebud Racing - the mechanic, Jock Ross, built a couple of air scoops on top of the wings to put air straight into the bottom of the car and the cockpit which made a great deal of difference.

"Jock Ross and I also took the cylinder heads of that car to Maranello at the end of '62 and had all the latest valve guide modifications done to them. I never won anything with that car, in fact most of the driving I did with it was at a disused airfield out near Victoria, Texas where Tom lived. We used to take the car out there and belt it round and round just for fun and Tom himself used to drive it them.

"I don't think the GTO 64s handled as well as the original cars I certainly didn't see any advantage. I don't remember thinking, 'Oh boy, this is good'."

DONALD McLEOD

"The GTOs were very reliable long distance cars and we also attached a great deal of importance to the shorter distance races. It was a question of how much publicity we got from racing. I'm certain we sold cars from the fact that we were in the public eye, racing and winning. After every single race the 'phone for the next two days was hot. All the owners would ring up, saying 'What happened, how did you get on?'

"It was unheard of to take spare engines or even spare gearboxes to races. For a race like Le Mans we just took along the component spares we thought we might need and that was it."

JACQUES SWATERS

"The GTO was one of the most reliable cars that Ferrari ever built for racing, much more reliable than the LM. It was a very strong car. Apart from the accidents, we had very few technical problems with the GTOs. I can't think of any real weakness on the car, certainly there was no problem with the engine. If you had good maintenance it was a very, very reliable car."

JOHN SURTEES

"The GTO was a very ordinary motor car. Because it was very ordinary and had no real good or bad points it became special. Whether you were Tom, Dick or Harry you could drive it reasonably well, not necessarily at the absolute optimum.

"It had no advanced technical features whatsoever. It was just an assembly of various parts that they had around. A rigid axle located reasonably well, standard Ferrari suspension and a standard three litre single camshaft V12.

"A very ordinary car that turned out to have quite a good shape aerodynamically, which obviously aided its handling, particularly at speed. I think that the flatter shape gave it more downforce which meant that it was more efficient than the Short Wheelbase. If I had to make a choice, I'd take the Short Wheelbase. I think that was a truly classic Ferrari because it was designed as a car. The GTO came about as a lot of pieces.

"The GTO was a nice friendly car to drive. It wasn't the most efficient of race cars but then we are talking about a period when you weren't racing against particularly efficient cars. Here was a strong car with a nice flexible power unit which could be driven hard and was very reliable. What more could you ask for? It was an ideal sort of customer car, it was like the Manx Norton customer racing machine in the early Fifties.

"In 1966 there were five GTOs lined up at the back of the Assistenze Clienti in Modena and if you had about £15,000 they would have been happy if you'd taken the whole lot away. They couldn't sell them, no one wanted them. If you'd rolled together every penny you could find and had bought them, in retrospect it would have set you up for life. The greatest growth you could possibly have had for the investment."

PETER SUTCLIFFE

"Half way through the 1965 season we had the heads off and decarbonised the engine but that was all we ever did, apart from changing brake pads, tyres, oils, adjusting and greasing it. As a private entrant's car the GTO was absolutely brilliant because you didn't have to take it to pieces after every race.

"Provided one had driven it within its rev limit and not run off the road, it required just routine maintenance. Apart from sets of points and plugs, I don't think we required any spares until the drop arm broke at Rheims."

ROY SALVADORI

"The GTO was certainly the easiest car to drive. You really had to push the Aston and throw it around. In the wet I would have thought you would have been much better off with the GTO. It was much smoother, the power would come in much easier, which is to be expected with a twelve.

"I think the GTO was probably the best GT car of all time, I find it very difficult to compare anything

with it, favourably. Significantly, anytime you compare cars with it such as the Aston, E Type or Cobra, you're comparing cars with a larger capacity engine."

DROGO SPECIAL
CHRISTOPHER KERRISON

"The body of the 250GT was damaged sufficiently in the accident at the 1962 Tourist Trophy to require a major rebuild. I had been impressed by the performance of the original Breadvan, it was quite patently quicker than the 250GTO. I remember seeing Abate driving it quickly and thinking whoever had done the work on it had made a good job of it.

"So I went out to Italy and discussed things with Neri and Bonaccini at their engineering 'shop in Modena and they said they though they could make some improvements to the chassis. I don't think that they came up with any engineering drawings as such, I think they just built the car as they saw fit.

"The body was designed by Bizzarini and built by Drogo. The work took about six months to complete over the winter of 1962-'63. The engine was moved back in the chassis, was converted to six 38 DCN Weber carburettors and the compression ratio was increased so that the engine produced the same horsepower as the GTO.

"Unfortunately there were some important things that were not done which if they had been would have made the car an awful lot quicker. It was a pity but I simply didn't have the amount of money required to do them. One was fitting a five speed gearbox which would have helped very much on short circuits. The other was that we didn't fit a Watts linkage, as had been introduced on the GTO.

"It required about fifteen hundred pounds to do the work and that seemed like a lot of money at the time, so I didn't spend it. I bitterly regretted it afterwards, because with that body in theory it could have gone a lot faster than the GTOs. When Michael Parkes drove the car, in one lap he managed to drive it faster than I had succeeded in doing. But I think he got out quite quickly, as I think he found it rather hairy himself!

"I drove it out of Neri and Bonaccini's workshop and through the streets to go and test it at the Modena circuit. Of course, it created a lot of attention, as it would do in Italy. There was a man riding along on

LAST LAP

a bicycle who saw it in the square in the middle of Modena, which it was necessary to cross to get to the track. He took both hands off the handlebars to blow a kiss at the car and promptly rode into a wall and fell off!

"The first time the car really performed well was at Spa. In practice I think we put up about the third fastest time overall which was quite a surprise as it was quicker than a lot of GTOs. That unquestionably demonstrated the effectiveness of the body which was lower and lighter than a GTO. Had we put in a five speed 'box and put the suspension right I think it would have been quicker. Compared with the GTO, it was much more difficult car to drive. When I finally got a GTO it was really like childs play driving it, there was such a difference between the two. The GTO was such an easy car to drive, it was terribly forgiving and really simple."

COBRA
PHIL HILL

"The Cobras had such limited suspension travel, if you put them on any kind of bumpy surface, they just couldn't hack it. At the Targa Florio, for instance, they spent most of the time in the air. They were predictable to a high degree but you had to know what they were capable of doing and allow for it."

INNES IRELAND

"Driving the Cobra at the Targa Florio was an experience. The car seemed to lurch from one bump on the road to the next. It was rather like having a 46 mile long accident."

ROY SALVADORI

"The Cobra was a weird car. It looked all wrong, more like a special but it handled surprisingly well. It was a car you really had to throw around, lots of grunt from the engine coming out of slower corners. If you had the thing lined up you had plenty of punch coming out of the corner which would give you an advantage. The first quarter of a mile out of a corner you were going great guns but it seemed to run out of steam, the higher you revved it. It had surprisingly good brakes.

"I really don't know what made the car work, but it was a good, safe car to drive, even if it didn't look that way at times. I had a Cobra for only two races in 1964. The Cobra wasn't the nicest car to drive but by then it was superior to the GTO."

JACK SEARS

"The Cobra's handling and brakes were poor by comparison to the GTO but the V8 engine made up for it by giving you a lot more grunt. The Cobra's acceleration over the first hundred yards was far quicker than the Ferrari and I used the power of the engine to the utmost and drove through the mishandling. The extra power was particularly useful on circuits where you would be accelerating out of slow corners, such as Druids at Brands Hatch.

"Driving a Cobra at the 1964 International Trophy meeting, I rather met my match with Graham Hill in the '64 GTO. We paced each other for the first three or four laps. His car was handling far better than mine and I realised that I couldn't hold him in the corners but if I used the power on the straights I could stay with him. After several laps of running close together I got off line and spun, proving to myself that the Cobra's real limitation was its handling."

JAGUAR E TYPE
PETER SUTCLIFFE

"The E Type was not really any nicer to drive than the GTO and one was more confident in the Ferrari engine. It really was just about unburstable, unless you were unlucky, whereas you had to be a bit more careful with the Jaguar because it did have one or two inherent problems, particularly with regard to the alloy block. They were both excellent handling cars and on its day an E Type could beat a GTO and frequently did in short distance races but very seldom in longer events. One never felt quite as confident that you could extend and thrash an E Type in a long event the way that you could a GTO.

"Handlingwise, there wasn't a lot to choose between the two. Brakes, gears and general handling on both were excellent. It was really just in the engine that the GTO scored."

JACK SEARS

"I felt the handling of the E Type never had the secure feel of the GTO. It was significantly better than the Cobra but the GTO felt like you could almost never get it out of line. On some circuits the E Type had an advantage accelerating out of tight corners. At Mallory Park in 1963 Graham Hill used the better torque of the E Type to beat my GTO. After a few laps I could see why Graham had chosen to race the E Type instead of the GTO. He would pull away from me coming out of the hairpin on almost every lap."

ASTON MARTIN
ROY SALVADORI

"There were no better brakes on any car than the Aston but unless you threw the Aston sideways through a corner, you weren't going to get anywhere. You had to drive it very hard and you had to get the back breaking away and try to get the car drifting. You would try to do it on all cars, you could do it with the GTO but it was more progressive, you'd start the Ferrari drifting and you could move it on the throttle but the only way you could get a time with the Aston was to check your steering and give it a bit of a snatch to get the back breaking away and then drive it in a drift.

"If you didn't do that, you weren't quick at all. That's why some drivers could never get to grips with it, because they didn't really understand how brutal you had to be. It didn't take me too long to adapt because I was a bit of a brutal driver and it suited my style, but for a delicate driver I would have thought it was a bit of an education. It was the way you had to drive to keep the thing on the cam. Then, of course, what do you do in the wet? ...you're in real trouble then.

"If you had to have a GTO or an Aston in a wet race you'd be very much better off with the GTO. The Aston rev range was fairly narrow, even on the big cars you only had 2300 - 2400 to play with. The Ferrari twelve cylinder engine's torque was so good and the rev range was much wider than the Aston's. You had plenty of power beginning at around 4500, with a range of 3000 - 3400 to play with.

"That made a lot of difference, the GTO engine was much more flexible and you didn't get the spit back that you did with the Weber carburettors on the Aston straight six. So you were able to play with the GTO much more, and not necessarily have to get down into a low gear, which would make things awkward.

"You didn't really want to take a corner like Lavant at Goodwood in second gear in the Aston, it was too low. In many cars the only way to get around a corner like that was to put your front wheel virtually off the road, get some wheelspin by getting the back moving then gently put your foot down to kill the wheelspin.

"With the Aston it was completely different, you'd throw it into the corner, get wheelspin but instead of putting your foot down coming out you would bring the throttle back until the revs equated to about 3600 r.p.m. when you would suddenly find it all gripping and you had plenty of poke. Then you would put your foot in it and come out of the corner drifting. But if you missed 3600 the carburettors would just spit. It was an unnatural way of driving.

"By being brutal with the Aston, Cobra and E Type you were really stressing the cars, far more than you would have to with the GTO. Often you'd wind up with broken spokes and wheels coming off because the cars were stressed so much.

"The Aston and Cobra did have more torque than the Ferrari but the GTO would make it up elsewhere, because it was so progressive, although there would have to be a point where the V12 would have to be at a disadvantage to a V8 or a straight six, which lower down would have to have more grunt, but also a narrow rev range."

MICHAEL SALMON

"The Aston was certainly much quicker in a straight line than the 250GTO. We had a lot of success with the car but it didn't prove to be nearly as reliable as we thought it was going to be. That Aston six cylinder engine was extremely good at short distance sprint races but it failed on the long distance time and time again. That was the big difference between the Aston and Ferrari.

"The Aston was very quick in practice and would start a long distance race going very quickly but the power would visibly taper off. It just wouldn't keep up to the performance that it would start the race with. For no particular reason it just used to dwindle whereas the GTO would either break or keep on going and going.

"The Aston appeared to have a fault in the centre of the engine with overheating and it used to burn pistons out. Although we never actually burnt one in the Project car in '64, we certainly did when we went to Le Mans in '62. All three cars went out with threepenny bit size holes in the pistons.

"The Aston was a car that could let you down and it was difficult to drive. I think they had possibly put the engine a little too far back in the chassis.

"The brakes were superior on the Aston, the GTO had weak brakes but because of its incredible handling ability they were perhaps not so vital as they would have been on a car that hadn't got the GTO handling qualities.

"On power, certainly the Aston was quicker because it produced an honest 310 b.h.p. and we used to see 325 b.h.p. on the dyno. Whether it was a very good engine or even not so good, it was substantially over 300 b.h.p. whereas the GTO produced about 285 - 290 b.h.p. So you had anything from 25 to 30 b.h.p. or more on the Aston and the power band was much wider.

"The peak revs of the Aston Martin were 6000-6200 r.p.m. and the Ferrari about 8000 - 8500. You had very little torque from the V12, there was a lot of power so long as you kept it right up there but the Aston was quicker in a straight line, very quick.

"The Aston was unstable in wet conditions, but if one was able to stay on the track with it, it was quicker. It was a car that could very easily turn round and bite you if you weren't firm with it. It was a clumsy, incompetent driver who would lose a GTO on a regular basis, they were just so forgiving it was unbelievable."

UNDER THE BONNET

RICHARD BIRKS

"The worst job on a GTO was changing the axle ratio, which was very time consuming. We didn't ever carry spare axles so we had to actually change the ratio in the axle. The rest of it was fairly easy, it was a very reliable car and really didn't give us a lot of trouble at all. Apart from the unusual breakage, like the end of the half shaft at the 'Ring, by and large the car was a delight from the mechanic's point of view, a wonderful machine to work on.

"Everything was reasonably easy to get at on the dry sump engine. As long as you changed the oil and plugs, put petrol in it and kept the filters clean it really was an easy car to look after. It wasn't heavy on brakes and it wasn't even particularly heavy on tyres.

"Unlike the Aston, we didn't have to warm the GTO up on soft plugs and then change onto hard plugs. The GTO would always crack up on the hard plugs, we always used to keep plenty of spares but it was never a question of having to change plugs. The Aston we would have to crack up on very, very soft plugs, warm it up and then change to much harder plugs.

"The Ferrari would start up very easily but it would take quite a long time to warm up because you had quite a lot of oil in the tank and you had to get that all nice and warm as well. Also we used to run a very thick oil in the axle, a viscosity of 2/40, so we used to put it up on jacks and warm the axle up. That was really quite important because the oil was like a thin grease."

JOHN MINNEY

"If the cars weren't damaged at all they'd be taken back to Poole Road and we'd just do a pre-race check. Obviously, if there was anything during the race that the driver had reported to us we would specifically look at that. We'd probably change the oil if it was dirty but we probably wouldn't change the spark plugs if everything was running o.k, they were those sort of cars.

"Provided the engine had been warmed up correctly and had been driven in a sensible manner when it wasn't being raced it would go for several events without even the plugs being taken out. We'd base the work we did on the cars between races on the reports that we got from the previous meeting.

"We'd obviously check the brake pads and safety items,

the road wheels and the spokes, make sure the tracking was o.k, check the clutch adjustment but it was really just general maintenance.

"We certainly wouldn't get into major work like engine overhauls, we only did that when we really had to. Depending on where the car was when the decision was made to do an engine rebuild, we would either do it at Poole Road or the car would go back to the factory.

"When we were first running the GTO we would decide before an event which axle ratio to run at a particular circuit. Sometimes in practice we would find that the car was pulling enough revs, or too many so we'd change the ratio again. We did that until we got to know which ratios were right for the car on a given circuit.

"How long it took depended on how much beer you'd had. You could change a rear axle and do the ratios in about five hours if you were reasonably sober. It was a difficult and rotten job that you had to do lying under the car. Setting it up was by means of shims and blueing it so that was by no means the happiest of jobs either.

"Then at the end of it all, you never knew if you'd got it perfectly meshed or not because the car was so noisy when it was running. If the axle itself was noisy on the overrun or in drive it didn't matter, you couldn't hear it anyway.

"Brake pads were pretty easy to change provided they came out and weren't seized in the runners. The front calipers were designed for quick changes with a single locating pin which you removed, then dragged the pads out. Provided the pistons went back O.K. you could change the front pads very quickly.

"The rears were more difficult because they didn't have the quick release mechanism which made them more difficult to get at. We'd probably be able to change all four front pads in about three quarters of a minute to a minute and the rears in about a minute and a half to a minute and threequarters.

"Sometimes in the UK the preparation of the car would be overseen by Florini, on other occasions we would do it ourselves. If the cars were being driven in Europe and there was sufficient time between races they would sometimes go to the Assistanze in Modena. Then we'd get a bill for the work. Frankly, I think we all used to be amazed with what used to be done on the cars. Sometimes I think we even perhaps wondered whether all the work had been done.

"We had some terrific bills, we all used to scratch our heads and say, 'My God!' and the Old Man used to go absolutely berserk. But I suppose when you look back, it was cheap motor racing, certainly nothing compared to today.

"The cars never went down to the factory burning excessive oil or with the head gaskets gone, or internal maladies on the engine. The factory had regular replacement cycles for parts like wheel bearings and clutch plates, which is fair wear and tear. I don't think there was any component that regularly failed on a GTO. What failures occurred were quite honestly insignificant in comparison with the overall reliability and design of the car.

"The cars we originally collected from the factory were fitted with Snap exhaust extractors. They were a good spoof: I have my doubts that they had any effect at all. They were supposed to work by air being forced through the outside of the extractor as the car moved, this helping accelerate the gas out of the tail pipe. They looked nice but I don't think they did anything in terms of performance. We used them in the early days of the GTO but they were left off the car after a time.

"You couldn't actually change the handling of the GTO a terrific amount. The thickness of the roll bar would make a difference, and you could tweak the Konis up or down a couple of turns. It was also possible to wind up the rear springs to a certain extent by putting a jack under the diff and putting a lot of weight in the rear of the body. This would reverse the semi-elliptical springs at the back but of course this would wear off during the course of a race.

"Otherwise, there really wasn't much you could do other than play with different front and rear wheel sizes but you couldn't do anything that would make a massive difference, unless it was something crazy like putting wide wheels at the front and narrow ones on the back.

"Of the drivers, unhappily, Graham was the least communicative as far as feedback went. You knew that once he got behind the wheel no one would drive harder or put more effort in, but as to actually helping you get more out of the car by good communication as to what was happening to the braking, steering, etcetera, dear old Graham was pretty hopeless. Once you'd got him behind the wheel, though, and the flag dropped, you'd got to put your money on him.

"Michael Parkes was quite easily the most interesting and the most helpful driver to work with. When he worked for the factory there would be some development stuff that he would pass on. Nothing of major significance, but every little tweek would help.

"You could always make a joint effort with Michael. If the car wasn't responding he would always give an indication of where we ought to be thinking about going. Graham's standard comment was, 'It's shitty' and you would say, 'Yes, but how and why?' and he would just scratch his nose and say, 'Well, it's just shitty'.

"Although we used to get pretty frustrated with him, we were one hundred percent behind him. Even when he used to win races in our cars he would still never admit that the car was good. The best you'd get was, 'Yeah, it was alright'. He did win us a lot of money and we loved him dearly but he was a bit of a bugger to work with.

"Very little happened to the GTO in the way of development. Apart from the rebodying in 1964 there were minor changes to the wheel cylinder and the road wheel sizes but the basic overall design of the car never changed. We were all quite excited at the prospect of the rebodied car but I think we all came to the conclusion that it offered very little advantage, if any.

"Ronnie Hoare was told by the factory to expect something quite exciting. He was quite happy to pay for it and although he never said he was disappointed, I think he was, as we all were. A lot of us felt that the route to go on the bodywork was the way David Piper went in lowering the roof rather than the shape the factory finally came up with.

"Nevertheless, we were the concessionaire and we had to wave the flag. If the factory said this was the latest and greatest, Ronnie was honour bound to get on and do the business with it. We would feed back information to the factory, as all the other concessionaires did and, of course, the cars would go back from time to time to be checked over but I don't think there was any development on the car. It didn't really need it. By the time the Cobra was up and running, I think the factory had lost interest in the GTO anyhow."